the

CANADIAN

CRAFT BEER

COOKBOOK

the

CANADIAN

CRAFT BEER

COOKBOOK

DAVID ORT

whitecap

Whitecap Books is known for its expertise in the cookbook market, and has produced some of the most innovative and familiar titles found in kitchens across North America. Visit our website at www.whitecap.ca.

EDITING: Theresa Best and Elizabeth McLean

COVER AND INTERIOR DESIGN: Andrew Bagatella

COVER PHOTOGRAPHY: Michelle Furbacher (background) and Robin Sharp (inserts)

FOOD PHOTOGRAPHY: Robin Sharp

FOOD STYLING: Rossy Earle

AUTHOR PHOTOGRAPH: Cheryl Bulpitt

PROFILE PHOTOGRAPHY: Brett Enquist (page 55), David Ort (page 79), Jennifer Roberts (page 95), Spinnakers Gastro Brewpubs and Guesthouses (page 145)

PROOFREADING: Eva van Emden

Printed in Canada

Library and Archives Canada Cataloguing in Publication

Ort, David, 1980-, author

    The Canadian craft beer cookbook / David Ort.

ISBN 978-1-77050-193-5 (pbk.)

1. Cooking (Beer)–Canada. 2. Food and beer pairing–
    Canada. 3. Microbreweries–Canada. 4. Cookbooks.
    I. Title.

TX726.3.O78 2013   641.6'230971   C2013-904143-5

The publisher acknowledges the financial support of the Government of Canada through the Canada Book Fund (CBF) and the Province of British Columbia through the Book Publishing Tax Credit.

13 14 15 16 17   5 4 3 2 1

ACKNOWLEDGEMENTS

It goes without saying that it takes a team effort to create a cookbook—until you actually do it and then the saying is the most important part. The creative, insightful and supportive people that I'm lucky enough to be surrounded by made this endeavour possible. My heartfelt thanks go to:

My partner, Cheryl Bulpitt, who handled the mountains of dirty dishes, the cross-country beer excursions and my all-consuming focus on this project with patience and support. All despite not drinking any of the beer herself.

All those friends and family who volunteered their time, energy and thoughtful expertise to help develop, test and taste the recipes, including Chris Cofield; Michael Di Caro; Suresh Doss; Karen, Andrew, Caitlin and Emma Jackson; Esther Katzman; Alex Nelson; Sheldon, Kim, Michelle, Kelly and Jason Ort; Vanessa Scott; Richard Sigesmund; Allison Slute; Joel Solish; and Zack Weinberg. My brothers, Mike and Steve, and their partners Ainslie Hancock and Leasha Schwab, who all have long experience tasting my kitchen experiments and finding ways to break it to me (gently) that they need fine-tuning.

Obviously, a cookbook about craft beer could not have been written without the delicious and creative product of hundreds of brewers. (I know a full glass definitely made the recipe-tasting part easier.) A special thanks to those breweries who have agreed to let us name their beers as suggestions. For the profiles I very much appreciated talking with Nicole Barry, Brad Clifford, Mirella Amato and Spinnakers Brewpub, and their patience with all of my questions.

The good folks at Whitecap and Fitzhenry & Whiteside, including Theresa Best, Elizabeth McLean, Michelle Furbacher, Nick Rundall and Sharon Fitzhenry, who steered this project (and me) through the process that takes an idea and makes it into a finished book.

A cookbook depends on recipe photos for a large part of its usefulness. I was happy to count on Rossy Earle to prepare, style and provide props for the recipes we shot. Robin Sharp took photos that surprised me with their quality and managed to capture the dishes at their best. They both are true professionals and I want to thank Robin and Rossy for their invaluable contributions to this cookbook.

And to my parents, who taught us to appreciate and be thankful for great food and engaging writing and to whom I dedicate this book.

CONTENTS

INTRODUCTION

Beer bubbles through the centre of many human civilizations. Historical accounts even suggest that beer is a primary reason people first settled in villages and took up agriculture on a permanent basis.

As one of our earliest alcoholic drinks (mead makes a claim for this title as well), beer has been at the heart of celebrations for millennia. It is by far the world's most popular alcoholic beverage, so chances are that when we toast each other's health or celebrate success, beer is in the glasses we clink together.

The alcohol in beer made it safer to drink and store than water. For centuries, beer was the only potable drink for many Europeans, and its importance gave it the status of a commodity. Governments involved themselves in its production and sale both to gather taxes and to protect its quality.

In the last 500 years, some people have had enough time and money to develop a taste for flavourful, not just potable, beers. Specialty beers are imported from all over the world, and beer aficionados also travel to the source to find their favourite brews. About 6 million people visit Munich's Oktoberfest every year (that's four times the city's population).

Naturally, as we've recognized that beer tastes great with food, we've noticed that it makes a stellar ingredient too. In long-established dishes, such as Welsh rabbit and Flemish beef stew, and more unconventional applications in ice cream or the icing for brownies, beer belongs on the plate as well as in the glass. With their diversity, craft beers bring a wide range of delicious flavours to recipes.

After more than four years of writing about food on my own site, foodwithlegs.com, I've noticed a common thread that runs through my recipes: I like the strong, fermented flavours that go well with flavourful beer. Cheese and pickles are two obvious examples, but there are also many dishes with briny, smoky, sweet or spicy flavours that pair much better with beer than any other drink. When I write about craft beer I can't help but focus on the characteristic flavours that complement and contrast those in food. All of the recipes that follow build on my experience with these complex, delicious flavours.

Many of the recipes go well together, and

RECOMMENDED BEERS

Each recipe in this book was devised with a specific style of beer in mind as an ingredient or an accompanying beverage, or both. Following the recipe, I've recommended a specific Canadian beer and sometimes an international beer as well.

Craft beer is almost always made on a relatively small scale and distribution is often concentrated on markets near the brewery to emphasize the local nature of the product, so you won't always be able to find one of the recommended beers. If you can't find the beer listed, look for another in that style. Even jumping between styles will often turn out well, but you need to consider the bitterness factor when the recipe involves cooking (see Cooking with Beer, page 11).

you could easily devise a menu by picking and choosing from various sections. In some cases I've also suggested dishes to pair with one another. Near the back of the book, you'll find recipes for Beer Cocktails, which pair nicely with many of the recipes in the Snacks section. The Pantry section will help you to get the most out of the main-course dishes.

I appreciate recipes that are based on thoughtful technique and thorough explanation—I hope I have succeeded in both cases. When developing and testing these recipes, I wanted to be sure that I was asking you to do things for supportable reasons. If you have a geeky aspect to your kitchen personality, I think you'll enjoy many of the recipes. That's not to say that you need to be very experienced or advanced to enjoy cooking with craft beer. This is an exciting time for craft beer lovers, and my hope for this book is that you'll use the recipes with your favourite craft beers and make them your own. Substitute, adapt and experiment, and let

me know about any great discoveries.

The following sections introduce you to the history of craft beer in North America, provide descriptions of different beer styles and the ingredients that go into making beer, and offer cooking tips to help you create great dishes every time.

A VERSATILE BEVERAGE

The selection of beers available to North Americans has come a long way since the dark ages of the 1970s when consumers were presented with a limited range of very similar products. Pale, flavourless, fizzy lagers still dominate many markets, but now they compete against hundreds of options that are produced on a smaller scale and made as flavourful as possible. This move to craft beer happened at different times around the world: from the formation of the Campaign for Real Ale in England in the early 1970s through the American microbrewery boom of the '80s and '90s, to a present where craft brewing is a growing industry in almost every country.

With the move away from interchangeable mass-produced lagers, we also drink beer differently. We've stopped exiling it to the garage fridge for hot summer afternoons cutting the grass or couch-bound duty in front of a game. Instead, craft beer drinkers appreciate its taste and drink it for an enjoyable experience. Even if we don't want beer that is just "a cold one," however, I think some beer drinkers still pause at the point of matching their beer with food.

The first and most obvious challenge is the dominance of other options, most notably wine. Wine producers, writers and fans have done a subtle job of building a default position for their side. The image of wine with dinner is carved deep into our shared cultural psyche. Wine is a fine drink that is often made with a great deal of skill and artistry, but, and I know I'm generalizing, it frequently strikes an awkward balance with food.

Cheese is one of the best examples of this imbalance. If you haven't been invited to at least one wine and cheese party in the last decade, I can only imagine that you live in a vegan, teetotalling commune. Cheese and wine sit smugly beside each other in our imagination as de facto partners. In reality, cheese has a fistful of sweet, lactic, funky, sharp and sour flavours that can make almost all wines taste harsh, or flat and pallid. Beer has malty sweetness for balance, a range of acidic and bright flavours for contrast, and hop bitterness to keep the palate interested. In addition, beer's carbonation fights butterfat's attempts to coat our mouths in flavour-blocking fat.

Sometime after the Second World War, North Americans expanded their diet beyond meat, potatoes, white bread and frozen peas. To go with the various Italian pasta dishes and French food, it seemed to make sense to serve the wines from those countries. That's a fine idea, but even when we make French or Italian dishes it's almost never the heavily sauced and butter-rich dishes from the classical canon. Furthermore, in my kitchen, I'm just as likely to reach for coconut milk and lemongrass as tomatoes and garlic when noodles are on for dinner. Beyond Thailand, dishes from Mexico, India, Korea, Japan and China (to make only a brief start on a long list) can all find an easy partner among the diversity of beer styles.

In addition to variety, beer's advantage as an ingredient is often its size. When recipes call for a quarter or half cup of wine, I feel my eyes start an automatic roll. That amount might be conveniently available, but it's just as likely that I'll skip opening a new bottle just to use one-twelfth of it. Half a cup from most beer bottles leaves a portion that is barely enough to keep thirst at bay while the cook slaves over the stove. After that, diners can choose their own beer, finding the match that works best for them.

WHAT IS CRAFT BEER?

This question was near the front of my mind as I wrote this book. Most lists of criteria for craft beer include such questions as: "How big is the brewery's production?" "Are they owned by an international conglomerate?" "Do they use adjuncts like rice and corn?" and "Do all (or most) of their products fit into one of the traditional beer styles?"

In the United States, the Brewers Association considers a brewery qualified to call itself a craft brewery if it produces less than 6 million barrels of beer per year, is no more than a quarter owned by another person or company who is not a craft brewer, and for at least half of its beer lineup uses adjuncts to "enhance rather than lighten flavour."

The size question is a thorny one because it is difficult to agree on where to draw the line. As American breweries such as Sierra Nevada and especially the Boston Beer Company (brewers of the Samuel Adams line) have grown, the "too big" limit has been notched progressively higher to keep them under the craft umbrella. Expansion of successful breweries is one of the reasons that we talk more of craft breweries than microbreweries these days.

Does beer know who owns the factory (or small storefront, repurposed warehouse or backyard) it was brewed in? Does craft beer necessarily change for the worse when a big company buys out a small competitor? (As Molson Coors did with Granville Island and Creemore Springs in Canada or Anheuser-Busch InBev did with Goose Island in Chicago.) Those questions are obviously cast to hook a "probably not" answer. But labels do matter. Many craft beer drinkers specifically want to connect with local entrepreneurs through carefully brewed beer. The best compromise solution I can find (that I did not invent) is to note in parentheses when a craft beer is owned by a conglomerate. So I'll write Traditional Pilsner—Creemore Springs Brewery (Molson Coors).

The way I see it, the use of cereal adjuncts is the most damning charge. There is only rarely a good "tastes better" reason to add rice and flaked corn in large quantities to beer. I admit that in my younger days I saw the bottom of more macrobrewed pale lagers than I want to count, but anyone who has switched to craft and goes back can't help but taste the thin, overly sweet and one-dimensional flavour of these commodity beers. But sometimes good beer does contain rice or corn, or sometimes a brewery makes a lot of mass-market lager and a little bit of really good craft beer. These are all examples of why the craft label needs to flex.

Arbitrating the question based on comparison to a list of accepted styles presents similar challenges to the scale of production issue. Who writes the list and decides the cut-off date for having invented traditional styles? This question is really more about the "beer" part than the "craft" part. I'm for a flexible, common-sense approach: a cidery is not producing craft beer, but if those who make gluten-free beer alternatives want to call their full-flavoured product "craft beer," I can't find a reason to deny them.

Once all of the easy objective criteria have been (mostly) set aside, what are we left with? I think we have to conclude that it's a fairly subjective question: craft is craft because it tastes good. It's made by brewers who care first about flavour rather than just consistency, cost or marketability—and who would choose to drink their own product. It's beer that doesn't need gimmicky advertising to distinguish it from competitors. Most of all, it's full-flavoured and delicious.

If you'd like to give craft beer homebrewing a shot, take a look at the Further Reading section for some excellent resources.

The American-based Beer Judge Certification Program (BJCP) published a guide to beer styles in 2008 that is widely accepted in North America. By design, the guidelines are meant for judges at homebrewing competitions to answer a question that is something like: Which of these entries best expresses the characteristics of the style? Judged competitions outside the US tend to have slight variations on their style definitions. Some professional brewers chafe at the idea of thinking about craft beer in reference to a set of rules and categories, preferring instead to say that they are brewing the most delicious beer they can.

For home cooks and consumers of craft beer, I think some classification is helpful. It's convenient to be able to go into a store that specializes in craft beer and ask for a category of beer, rather than just one particular label.

This list of styles, while not as comprehensive as the BJCP guidelines, describes the general characteristics of the beers you'll need for the recipes in this book.

Lagers

Lagers were developed as a group of styles in central Europe during the 19th century. They are all brewed with yeasts that ferment at the bottom of the tank (these are cultured strains of brewer's yeast that prefer cooler temperatures). In general, they are lighter in colour, body and flavour than ales and should be served at cooler temperatures. There are craft beers in a variety of lager styles, but the category also includes the mass-market international lagers that dominate the global beer market.

Pilsner

This style traces its origins to Bohemia and the surrounding area in southern Germany and specifically, to Pilsen in the Czech Republic. Pilsners tend to be quite hoppy and pale in colour.

Bock

These smooth lagers are medium to dark in colour and have a low level of bitterness. **Doppelbocks** have a relatively higher alcohol content and more malt sweetness.

Märzen

Märzen are strong, somewhat hoppy beers that were traditionally brewed in Germany in March and designed to keep during the warm summer months. The strongest, hoppiest examples would last until the end of September when they were served as **Oktoberfest** beers.

Dark lager

Sometimes also known as **schwarzbiers**, these dark lagers are brewed with some dark, roasted malt in the recipe. The style comes from what used to be East Germany, and it only barely survived the 20th century.

Smoked lager

~~The malt used to make smoked beers is smoke-~~ dried over wood fires. Bamburg, Germany, is the style's traditional centre, where they are usually known as **rauchbier.**

Ales

Ales are the older of the two general styles of beer-making and use top-fermenting yeasts, which act quickly at warmer temperatures than lager yeasts. In general, ales should also be served at a warmer temperature than lagers.

Abbey ale

If the beer is brewed by one of the eight designated Trappist monasteries in Europe that brew beer, it can use the protected Trappist designation. **Dubbels** are strong and have lots of dark and dried fruit flavours. **Tripels** are stronger still, but tend to be paler and lean more to rum-like spice flavours. Other monasteries (and non-monastic brewers) around the world also make beers that mimic the characteristics of these styles.

Belgian witbier

This style is brewed with a particular Belgian yeast and tends to have a light colour and flavour. Witbiers usually show flavours of orange peel and coriander (often because those are ingredients).

Saison and bière de garde

These ales from southern Belgium and northern France, respectively, are light gold to orange in colour and match fruity, yeast-derived aromas with a subtle bitter kick. **Bières de garde** usually have more of an herbal spice note than **saisons.** Both go exceptionally well with a wide variety of food.

Brown ales

Amber to dark brown in colour, **English brown ales** are low in bitterness and can be high in malt sweetness. Their roasted flavours go well with the flavour of roasted or grilled meat. **American brown ales** tend to be quite hoppy by comparison to the English ones.

Pale ale

Not to be confused with commercial pale lagers, pale ales are brewed from malts on the lighter end of the spectrum, but also prominently feature hops, which make them some of the most strongly flavoured beers. **English-style pale ales** depend on hops for bittering and a floral, complex aroma, while their **American-style pale ale** cousins (which grew out of the craft-brewing industry in the Pacific Northwest) are even more bitter and go for bright citrus flavours, such as grapefruit peel, from their hops. **Belgian-style pale ales** strike a balance between the English and American styles and put yeast-derived aromas and flavours in the spotlight. **India pale ales** (IPAS) have a historical connection to ales—they were brewed with a higher level of alcohol and more hops to preserve them for the journey to India during the British colonial period there. Again, IPAS in the American style tend to have more citrus-flavoured hops than the English style. A beer that is marketed as an "Imperial" version of any of the sub-styles of pale ale will be higher in alcohol and hop bitterness.

THE G WORD: GLUTEN

I know that many people, on the combined advice of their doctors and digestive systems, don't eat food with gluten. That's a bit of a challenge for a cookbook about beer because the four grains most likely to be in beer are barley, wheat, oats and rye, and they all form at least a little bit of gluten when combined with water.

In the last few years, some brewers have started to make gluten-free beer with sorghum, millet, rice, corn and quinoa. My thoughts after tasting these have landed somewhere between "atrocious" and "mediocre." This is beginning to change, and brewers such as Montreal's Brasseurs Sans Gluten are starting to catch up. They swept the gluten-free category at the 2012 World Beer Cup.

The bottom line is that in many cases a gluten-free beer will be just fine as a substitution in recipes, but you should be sure to use one that you would be happy to drink on its own.

Porter and stout

These related beer styles are marked by the dark colour they get from roasted malt. Along with the colour, they often share flavours like chocolate, coffee and dark toast. **Imperial porters** and **imperial stouts** both have a higher alcohol level than usual and generally have a thicker mouth feel.

Barley wine

These medium- to dark-coloured beers have a complex mix of flavours and a lot of alcohol. The history of the barley-wine style stretches back to Norman times. Nobles living in England who couldn't grow grapes but wanted to imitate their favourite drink managed to do so by using the materials available to them. That connection and the higher alcohol level is the reason these beers are called wines. **American-style barley wines** usually have more hops (and bitterness) to balance their malty sweetness compared to **English-style barley wines.**

Weissbier

Wheat is used as well as malted barley to make these light-coloured ales. **Hefeweizen** have a cloudy appearance caused by the unfiltered yeast, which also gives them their distinctive aromas and flavours of banana and cloves. They are the most popular style of beer in Bavaria. Strong weissbiers are known as **weizenbocks.**

Sour beers

In Belgium, the brewers of lambic beer (and its cousins kriek, framboise and gueuze) use wild fermentation or cultured strains of bacteria (often *Lactobacillus*) and yeast (usually a species of *Brettanomyces*) to make beers that are tart and acidic. **Sour Flemish red** and **oud bruin** are sour styles defined by their colour.

Other ales

Spiced ales, winter ales and **Christmas ales** add seasonal spices and other flavourful ingredients to an ale base. The spice theme continues with **pumpkin ales** that show notes of the familiar pumpkin pie spices.

Scotch ales tend to be very low in hops and high in malt flavour.

Oak-aged ales have been laid down in oak barrels or casks, from which they pick up complex flavours, including vanilla and spices. They are usually quite high in alcohol.

Smoked ales are made with smoke-dried malt, similar to the process for smoked lagers. Smoke is a very strong flavour that tends to dominate.

Other Styles

Kölsch

Kölsch is a style with one foot in both the ale and lager camps. Brewers choose whether to use ale or lager yeast and then ferment the beer at a temperature halfway between what is usual for lagers and ales. Hops are prominent in this style, but it's not particularly bitter.

Ginger beers

Ginger beers don't use malt or hops in the recipe, but a particular colony of bacteria and yeast culture ferments the sugars found in ginger to create alcohol and carbonation. If the fermentation is stopped at an early stage, non-alcoholic ginger beer is produced.

BEER INGREDIENTS

When I was developing the recipes for this book, I wanted to do more than just take a good recipe that called for using another liquid (wine, sherry, milk or water) and create an adapted recipe by substituting beer. In each case, I considered the existing recipe and asked myself: What is beer going to add?

But that in turn raised another question: What flavours does beer contribute? The best way to answer this question is to consider beer flavours through the lens of the ingredients typically found in beer. Here they are, with a list of their associated flavours.

Grains

Speaking very simply, beer is made by cooking malted grain with water to make a sweet liquid called wort, whose sugar can be fermented into alcohol by yeast. Hops and other ingredients are added later for colour, flavour and preservation.

To convert their starches into fermentable sugar, cereal grains (usually barley) are forced to partly germinate. In a process called malting, hot air is applied to the grain to stop the sprouting. To give the final beer a variety of flavours, aromas and colours, the grain, now called green malt, is kilned to a specified shade, including pale, crystal, amber, chocolate and black malt. In some cases, unmalted grain is mixed with malted for flavour and colour, and to help create the foamy head we look for on a glass of beer.

Barley makes up the majority of most grain bills (the grain part of a beer recipe, also sometimes called "the grist"), followed by wheat, oats and rye. Large-scale commercial brewers often use corn and rice for their pale lagers because they are cheap and create a consistent, sweet, inoffensive product that suits the lowest common denominator of palates.

The list of flavours that beer gets from grain includes roasted coffee, chocolate, sweet, biscuity, caramel, spicy, peppery, smoky and bread-like.

Hops

Hops are the cone-shaped female flowers of the *Humulus lupulus* plant. They were once added to beer for flavour and also as a preservative. Now that we have refrigeration that is more convenient than alpine caves, the focus is on aroma and flavour. Generally speaking, the light and snappy bitterness of hops balances the heavy, rich sweetness of malts.

Dozens of varieties of hops are grown commercially, and their contribution to a finished beer changes according to two characteristics. A hop variety that is higher in what are called alpha acids will contribute bitterness to a beer's flavour; one higher in beta acids will give aroma.

Beers that are made in an "American style" (like pale ales and barley wines) tend to use American hops, which usually have more bitterness than their British counterparts.

From hops, beer gets bitter, citrus, grapefruit, orange, pine, cedar and resin flavours, and also all of these as aromas.

Yeast

Brewer's yeast

Brewer's yeast (*Saccharomyces cerevisiae*) creates two important by-products when it metabolizes fermentable sugars in what will become carbon dioxide and pure alcohol. The carbon dioxide gives beer its fizz and head, which both have significant effects on how we perceive flavours and aromas. Alcohol does more than just intoxicate; it has its own flavour and aroma as well as antimicrobial properties, which made beer safer than water for a large chunk of human history. As an ingredient in cooked dishes, alcohol has the special ability to dissolve certain flavours that are beyond the reach of water. For instance, some flavour compounds in tomatoes only become perceptible when dissolved in alcohol.

Yeast fermentation also produces a long list of complex compounds—mostly volatile, fragrant chemicals called esters—that occur in small amounts but make an outsized contribution to a beer's flavour and aroma. Each strain of yeast can potentially create its own specific cocktail of aromas and flavours, so the yeast's origin is an important consideration when predicting how a beer will taste. Brewers spend a great deal of effort and money creating (and protecting) their own strains of brewer's yeast. Belgian beers (and those made in a Belgian style) tend to shine more light on the yeast's characteristics than beers that depend on hops or malt for their flavour.

When we taste or smell flavours in beer that are bready, banana-like, funky, musty and complex, they usually are from yeast.

Wild yeast and bacteria

Contemporary brewers almost always make their beer by adding cultured brewer's yeast to the sweet liquid (wort) that is drained (sparged) from the mix of malted grain in a tightly controlled and carefully sanitized environment. Under these conditions, brewer's yeast is pretty much the only microbial game in town. Before yeast was isolated and produced in a lab, however, traditional brewers cultured their beer either with the previous batch's foamy residue or by depending on the spontaneous action of wild yeast.

Wild-fermented beers are particularly interesting because *Brettanomyces* (from Latin for "British fungus" and often just called "Brett") and *Lactobacillus* (a "good" bacteria) are also active in the beer, and they produce acetic and lactic acids that lend a tart edge and a pleasant mouth-puckering sensation.

Sour beers can be difficult to produce (and some brewers worry that the wild yeast and bacteria might contaminate the rest of their brewing operations), sometimes require special bottles, and taste noticeably different than what most consumers expect. All those factors mean that sour beers can be difficult to find, but they are stellar choices from a food perspective. Their acidity cuts through fat and spice, and the unusual flavours match well with some of my favourite foods, such as dry-cured sausage, blue cheese and sourdough bread.

Beers fermented with wild yeasts and bacteria tend to taste sour, tart or acidic, and may be described as having barnyard, funky or horse blanket flavours. Some of their complex flavours are acquired tastes, sought after by aficionados.

Water

By volume, water is always the main ingredient in any beer. Professional and even homebrewers give a great deal of thought and attention to how their water tastes and how its chemistry and percentage of dissolved solids will affect the brewing process.

For recipes, we have to worry less about those variables and generally, because water is nearly flavourless, we're more concerned with cooking it away. As discussed in Beer in the Recipe Ingredients section below, cooking causes water to evaporate and concentrates bitter compounds.

One strong caveat: Beware of overdoing the bitterness when cooking with beer. As the liquid in a cooked dish reduces because the water evaporates, the original level of bitterness in the beer will concentrate, sometimes beyond what is palatable. I have found that 20 IBUS and below is almost always safe for reductions. Up to about 40 IBUS should be used with caution, and I'd only go above that rarely.

Wild Cards

A difference between beer and wine is that brewers who want their beer to include a particular flavour (cherries, for instance) can go ahead and add that ingredient. These added ingredients are called adjuncts. Even the most traditional Belgian witbiers often contain spices and Curaçao orange peel. Some chocolate stouts actually have chocolate, and milk stouts add milk powder.

Maple syrup, coffee, honey, bacon, oysters, mustard seeds, bananas, chamomile, rose hips, peanuts, chilies, vanilla beans and jasmine flowers are only a small sample of the list of unusual ingredients that make their way into a brew kettle somewhere.

RECIPE INGREDIENTS

Beer

Beer is an ingredient in most of the recipes in this book. Because it is such a varied and complex product, including it in a recipe is really like adding five ingredients: water, malt, carbon dioxide (and in unpasteurized beers, the live yeast that created it), alcohol and bitterness. Obviously, as a liquid, beer is mostly water. It combines with the protein in flour to form the gluten that gives baked goods their texture. Beer's carbonation adds gas to batters and doughs to leaven them. The bitterness that beer gets from hops is a welcome balance for sweet flavours in recipes.

Hops

Hops come in both pellet and whole leaf form. For cooking, pellet hops are generally easier to use. Homebrewing supply companies are the best source for hops.

Spent Grain

The drained, mashed grain left over from the brewing process is known as "spent grain." Much of the sugar will have dissolved into the wort, but the spent grain retains some of its flavour and all of its dietary fibre. If you don't produce your own spent grain, you may be able to get some from a nearby brewery or ask a homebrewer friend for some.

Flour

When recipes call for "flour," they mean all-purpose flour. Bread flour will be specified by name. You can almost always substitute all-purpose for bread flour, especially in Canada, where good-quality all-purpose flour is almost as high in protein.

Salt

My recipes usually use kosher salt, and I prefer the Diamond Crystal brand. It's worth seeking out this brand because it doesn't have any iodine or anti-caking agents and the crystal shape and size are just right for sprinkling and seasoning meat.

Sugar

If a recipe calls for just "sugar," it means white granulated sugar. Other types such as dark brown sugar will be specified.

Eggs

For egg yolks, whites and whole eggs, use only large eggs.

Rice Flour and Rice Bran Oil

Given that craft brewers generally shun rice as an ingredient, it's a bit ironic that a few of my recipes call for its use. Unlike wheat flour, rice flour doesn't form gluten when combined with water, so it makes for especially light and tender batters. Most grocery stores or bulk stores carry rice flour, but if you can't find it, you can substitute all-purpose flour.

The idea to use rice bran oil for deep-frying comes from *Ideas in Food* by Aki Kamozawa and H. Alexander Talbot. It reaches a higher temperature without breaking down, and I find it makes deep-fried food with a delicious, golden-brown crust. Best of all, it smells like a pleasant carnival midway rather than a greasy fish 'n' chips shop. The Alfa One brand is becoming more widely available in Canada. If you can't find rice bran oil, use sunflower, peanut or canola oil.

COOKING TIPS

Measuring by Weight

There are several good reasons to measure ingredients by weight rather than volume. The first and probably most important is that the results will be more accurate. The best example of this is all-purpose flour, one cup of which can vary between 4 and over 4½ ounces (125 and 140 grams). Brown sugar and shredded or grated cheese are two ingredients whose amount can vary drastically based on how tightly they're packed into the measuring cup. In both cases it's easier to buy the right amount (or see if you already have it) if you know how much you need by weight.

I hope we can make a simple bargain: if you'll at least consider buying a $30 kitchen scale, I'll build the recipes that follow so that the $400 stand mixer is optional.

All that said, recipes in this book only list weight measures as an option. There is always a volume or count alternative. If you want to measure flour by the cupful, use a large spoon or second cup to scoop the flour into the cup measure and then level it with the back of a knife or other straight edge. This will give a cupful of flour that usually weighs about 4 ½ ounces (about 140 grams).

Special Equipment
Pots
Recipes in this book that involve deep-frying or braising call for using an enamelled, cast iron Dutch oven. In most cases you can use a stockpot that has a heavy, clad-metal bottom and a tight-fitting lid.

European-made Dutch ovens (by Le Creuset or Staub) can be very expensive, but based on their durability, aesthetics and utility might be worth the cost. Lodge (an American manufacturer of cast iron) makes a line that is less expensive and only slightly less foolproof. For deep-frying, a plain black cast iron Dutch oven will work just fine, but may leach iron into acidic braising liquids.

Mixers
A stand mixer is listed as an optional tool for some of the recipes, but you'll be just fine if you only have a hand-held mixer (or even a whisk and bowl, in many cases).

Top-of-the-line blenders are powerful tools that come with a price to match. An immersion or stick blender will do just fine for all these recipes. Some recipes call for a food processor; for those, a blender or lots of knife work are passable substitutes.

Digital kitchen scale
Every kitchen should have this essential item, as I argue in Measuring by Weight, above. They make cooking more accurate and convenient and also are essential for related hobbies such as home brewing.

Thermometers
The temperature of a pot of hot oil or a piece of medium-rare fish is not worth estimating. A high-quality, instant-read probe thermometer can be used to accurately measure the temperature of many things, ranging from fish fillets to steaks to deep-frying oil.

DEEP-FRYING

I hope we can agree to put two misconceptions about deep-frying behind us, namely, that it is difficult and dangerous to do at home. It's not difficult with the right tools and a solid recipe. There are, however, some common-sense precautions that you should take to reduce the limited danger:

- Never leave a pot of hot oil unattended.
- Always know where your fire extinguisher is and that it is in good working order.
- Have a lid standing by to cover the pot of hot oil in an emergency.
- Don't overload the pot. The moisture escaping from frying food will bubble vigorously.

COOKING WITH ALCOHOL

It's a kitchen myth that alcohol will quickly evaporate when heated and the cooked dish will have none in it. A study conducted by the University of Idaho, Washington State University and the USDA found that even when alcohol vapours are flamed (as in flambé), about three-quarters of the alcohol is left in the dish. After two and a half hours of simmering or braising in the oven, 5 percent of the alcohol will still not have evaporated. This means that those who need to avoid all alcohol should not use beer in their recipes.

If you're concerned about feeding alcohol to children, make your own decision, but take a couple of numbers into account. Depending on the cooking method and time, between 20 and 90 percent of the alcohol will evaporate. As well, a quarter cup of 5-percent beer has less alcohol than 2 teaspoons of pure vanilla extract.

Ice cream maker

While it's definitely possible to make the ice cream recipes in this book without an ice cream maker, if you want to make these frozen desserts a regular part of your rotation, you'll probably want to invest in one.

DRINKING CRAFT

Craft beer is a delicious ingredient in recipes, but it will always be a drink first. Here are two general rules for getting the most enjoyment from drinking craft beer.

Use a glass

Beer comes into our homes in glass bottles or metal cans. These containers are designed to exclude light and oxygen and to retain carbonation (cans are better than bottles on all three counts). They are storage containers rather than serving vessels.

Carbonation wants to be released, and beer is meant to have a foamy head on it, which only forms when you pour out the beer. Furthermore, beer that's been poured out won't make you feel unpleasantly full and bloated.

In addition, brewers pay careful attention to their beer's clarity, colour and general appearance. Opaque aluminum or coloured glass won't let you fully appreciate how beautiful your beer is.

Now that we're using a glass, the question becomes which glass? The full list includes flutes, steins, snifters, tulips, chalices, pilsner glasses, stanges and weizen glasses. Each style of beer goes best with one or two shapes of glassware.

Naturally, not everyone will want to collect enough of each glass style to host a party. If you're having friends over for a tasting, bring out your largest wine glasses. They will trap the beer's aroma and head and display its appearance. Wine etiquette calls for drinkers to hold their glasses by the stem, but because most beer benefits from the warmth of a little hand-to-glass contact, large stemless wine glasses are another good option.

Serve at the right temperature

A gimmick on the outside of a beer can that indicates when it is "ice cold" is really just an indication that the beer inside will be terrible.

Good beer needs to be served at a temperature between 41°F and 55°F (5°C and 13°C). Many craft beers now come with a recommended serving temperature printed on the can.

SNACKS

When planning a multi-beer evening, be it pints at the pub or a beer-tasting party, it's best to progress from the least to the most intense beer. The challenge is that malt, alcohol, hop bitterness and sourness need to be taken into account at the same time.

Some of the dishes in this first section use heavier, higher-alcohol beers as an ingredient. Feel free to save the rest of the bottle for later in the evening.

Guacamole

RECOMMENDED BEER
American-style India pale ale
Hop Head, Tree Brewing (British Columbia)

SERVES 6-8

PREPARATION TIME 15 minutes, plus 1 hour for flavours to meld

2 ripe avocados, pitted

⅓ cup (80 mL) American-style India pale ale

3 Tbsp (45 mL) lime juice, freshly squeezed

2 plum tomatoes, quartered, cored and diced

¼ red onion, finely diced

½ tsp (2.5 mL) ground cumin

¼ tsp (1 mL) cayenne

kosher salt

MASHED AVOCADO HAS a silky texture and rich flavour that go well with the punch of a hoppy India pale ale. Tomatoes add some sweetness and a hint of acid that bring the flavours together. If plum tomatoes aren't in season, use an equivalent amount of cherry tomatoes. Serve with tortilla chips.

Cut the avocado flesh into large chunks with the tip of a sharp chef's knife. Scoop the flesh out of the skin and transfer to a small mixing bowl. Toss with the beer and lime juice. Mash with a potato masher until it is almost smooth. Add tomatoes, onion, cumin, cayenne and kosher salt.

Guacamole is best served at cool room temperature and needs an hour after being mixed for the flavours to come together. If you make it ahead or want to store leftovers, place a piece of plastic wrap directly in contact with the surface of the guacamole. The only way to stop it from browning is to keep it away from air. (The acid in the lime juice also helps.) The idea that sinking the pits into the dip does anything is a kitchen myth. If anything, they probably hurt by lifting the plastic wrap away from the surface of the guacamole.

DIP

RECOMMENDED BEER
Pilsner
Pilsner, Steam Works Brewing (British
    Columbia)

SERVES 6–8

PREPARATION TIME 10 minutes

....

2 garlic cloves, peeled

one 14-oz (398 mL) can artichoke
hearts, drained

14–18 niçoise olives, pits removed

1 oz (30 g) grated good-quality
Parmesan cheese (about
¼ cup/60 mL)

3 anchovy fillets

2 tsp (10 mL) fennel seeds, crushed

4 sprigs thyme, leaves stripped

juice and zest of half a lemon

freshly ground black pepper

¼ cup (60 mL) pilsner

¼ cup (60 mL) extra-virgin olive oil

STEAMED GLOBE ARTICHOKES dipped in butter make a fascinating dish, but breaking down artichokes at home for a dip is a fairly arduous task. Good-quality canned artichoke hearts will do just fine. On the other hand, be sure to buy olives that still have their pits. Remove the pits by gently smashing the olives with the flat side of a chef's knife and then working the pits out with your fingers.

This dip works just as well spread on lightly toasted sourdough or as a sauce for roasted potatoes.

———— ❧ ————

Put the garlic cloves into the bowl of a food processor and blitz until finely chopped. Add the artichoke hearts, olives, cheese, anchovies, fennel seeds, thyme leaves, lemon zest and juice, and a couple of grinds of black pepper. Process until a chunky paste forms. With the machine running, pour the beer and olive oil into the feed tube. Stop the food processor when they have been integrated.

Taste the dip. The olives and anchovies will probably have made it salty enough, but adjust the seasoning to suit your taste. You may also have to add more lemon juice for the proper hit of acidity.

MARINATED OLIVES

RECOMMENDED BEER
Abbey tripel
La Buteuse, Microbrasserie Le Trou
    du Diable (Quebec)
Tripel Karmeliet, Brouwerij Bosteels
    (Belgium)

SERVES 8

PREPARATION TIME 10 minutes,
plus 1–3 days to marinate

COOKING TIME 10–12 minutes

small container mixed olives with
pits, about 1 cup (250 mL)

½ cup (125 mL) abbey tripel

1 sprig rosemary, leaves stripped
from the stem, minced

freshly ground black pepper

WITH TWO VERY easy steps and a bit of time, the olive goes from ingredient to great-tasting (and fancy-looking) appetizer. This recipe is much better with bulk olives (rather than jarred or canned) and many better grocery stores now have an olive bar. An olive's size, shape, degree of ripeness when picked, and how it was treated all affect its flavour. This recipe does best when a mixed bag is used. Happily, most olive bars have a bin with an "olive medley." Also look for ones that still have their pits. Pitted olives seem to lose their meaty texture and take on an astringent flavour.

Serve as a pre-dinner snack with the same beer you use in the marinade.

———————— ❧ ————————

Dump the olives into a small mixing bowl. Don't throw away the container they came in. Add the other ingredients and stir to combine. Return olives and the marinade to their container or another non-reactive container. Refrigerate for 1 to 3 days.

Heat your oven to 350°F (175°C); set a rack in the middle position.

Take the olives from the refrigerator and drain the marinade. Transfer them to an ovenproof dish. (Bonus points if it also happens to be a small casserole that can act as a serving dish.) Place the dish in the oven for 10 to 12 minutes or until the olives are warm to the touch.

Beer Nuts

RECOMMENDED BEER
Porter
Pothole Porter, Half Pints Brewing
  (Manitoba)

SERVES 8–10

PREPARATION TIME 10 minutes

COOKING TIME 30 minutes, plus
at least 2 hours to cool

....

2¾ oz (82.5 g) brown sugar, lightly
packed (about ⅓ cup/80 mL)

⅓ cup (80 mL) granulated sugar

8 Szechuan peppercorns, crushed in
mortar and pestle (optional)

1 dried lime, crushed in mortar
and pestle

¼ tsp (1 mL) cayenne

½ Tbsp (7.5 mL) fine sea salt

14 oz (400 g) peanuts, blanched and
unsalted (about 2½ cups/625 mL)

1 egg white

4 tsp (20 mL) porter

THERE ARE A COUPLE of ingredients on the list below that might not already be in your kitchen. They really should be. Szechuan peppercorns combine a bit of heat with that unique tongue-numbing tingle. Dried limes are one of the few ways to add a sour-citrus flavour without adding liquid. They have lots of applications, for example, in Persian stews and as a cocktail ingredient. If you absolutely can't find both, the peppercorns can be omitted and a tablespoon (15 mL) of freshly squeezed lime juice can stand in for the dried.

———— ≫✺≪ ————

Heat your oven to 275°F (140°C); set a rack in the middle position. Line a cookie sheet with parchment paper or a silicone mat.

Combine the sugars, Szechuan peppercorns, dried lime, cayenne and sea salt in a medium mixing bowl. In a larger bowl, whisk together the egg white and porter. Add the peanuts and toss to coat with the egg white and beer mixture.

Bake on the cookie sheet for 30 minutes. Stir once or twice to keep the nuts from burning and sticking together too badly. After removing from the oven, use the paper or mat as an impromptu funnel to pour the nuts onto a plate and leave them to cool for 15 minutes. Break apart into bite-sized chunks and allow to cool fully before serving. If making ahead or if you have leftovers, store the nuts in a tightly sealed container.

NOTE The fine sea salt gives an even distribution and sticks better to the peanuts than larger, heavier flakes. Table salt is an acceptable (if not ideal) substitute.

Beer Nuts

RECOMMENDED BEER
Smoked ale
Holy Smoke Scotch Ale, Church-
    Key Brewing (Ontario)

SERVES 8–10

PREPARATION TIME 10 minutes

COOKING TIME 30 minutes, plus
at least 2 hours to cool

....

5¼ oz (157.5 g) brown sugar, lightly
packed (about ⅔ cup/160 mL)

¼ tsp (1 mL) cayenne

½ Tbsp (7.5 mL) fine sea salt

1 egg white

1 Tbsp (15 mL) maple syrup

4 tsp (20 mL) smoked ale

14 oz (400 g) almonds
(about 3 cups/750 mL)

I HAVE INCLUDED TWO recipes for spiced nuts to make a couple of points. First, at least in this case, the particular nuts you use are fairly interchangeable. If you can't find almonds or really lovely pecans, go ahead and substitute. Second, for the Sweet and Sour Beer Nuts (page 21), the beer plays a supporting role. In this case, the smoky rauchbier-style smoked ale will be one of the first flavours that most people notice.

As with the choice of nuts, feel free to adjust the seasoning blend to suit your preferences.

———— ❧ ————

Heat your oven to 275°F (140°C); set a rack in the middle position. Line a cookie sheet with parchment paper or a silicone mat.

Combine the brown sugar, cayenne and sea salt in a medium mixing bowl. In a larger bowl, whisk together the egg white, maple syrup and ale. Add the almonds and toss to coat with the egg white and ale mixture.

Bake on the cookie sheet for 30 minutes. Stir once or twice to keep the nuts from burning and sticking together too badly. After removing from the oven, use the paper or mat as an impromptu funnel to pour the nuts onto a plate, and leave them to cool for 15 minutes. Break apart into bite-sized chunks and allow to cool fully before serving. If making ahead or if you have leftovers, store the nuts in a tightly sealed container.

NOTE The fine sea salt gives an even distribution and sticks better to the peanuts than larger, heavier flakes. Table salt is an acceptable (if not ideal) substitute.

scallion pancakes

RECOMMENDED BEER
Amber ale
Thirsty Beaver Amber Ale, Tree
    Brewing (British Columbia)

SERVES 4

PREPARATION TIME 40 minutes

COOKING TIME 5-7 minutes per
pancake

....

4 oz (125 g) flour (1 cup/250 mL
less 1 Tbsp/15 mL)

4 oz (125 g) rice flour
(scant ⅔ cup/160 mL)

pinch kosher salt

1⅓ cups (330 mL) amber ale,
very cold

2 eggs, lightly beaten

1 Tbsp (15 mL) sunflower oil
(or other neutral oil)

4 scallions, cut diagonally
into slivers

1 tsp (5 mL) sunflower oil

As A KID ONE of my greatest dinner thrills came when we had pancakes for dinner. They were always the regular, slightly sweet breakfast pancakes, just served at a rebellious-feeling hour. These traditional Korean pancakes are savoury by nature. The scallion version has done the best job of making the jump onto the North American menus, but this batter can serve as a canvas for many other vegetables. Grated carrots or slivered zucchini are good, diced and sautéed mushrooms are better, but chopped kimchi is the best alternative to the classic.

Scallion pancakes (or any of the mentioned variations) are ideal accompaniments for fried chicken or pulled pork. Or eat them as a snack, with soy sauce for dipping.

The beer's carbonation gives the pancakes a slight lift. It's best to make the batter right before you want to cook the pancakes so that the gas doesn't dissipate.

Heat your oven to 250°F (120°C); whisk both flours and the salt together in a medium mixing bowl. Add the beer, eggs and oil and whisk to form a smooth, lump-free batter. Fold in the sliced scallions.

Heat a medium non-stick pan with 1 teaspoon (5 mL) of oil over medium heat for 2 to 3 minutes or until the oil starts to shimmer. Ladle about a quarter of the batter into the pan. Lift the pan and swirl it to coat the bottom of the pan evenly. Cook the pancake undisturbed for 3 to 4 minutes or until the batter looks like it has set. Check the bottom of the pancake and if it is dark brown in spots, use an offset spatula to flip it to the other side. Cook on the second side for 2 to 3 minutes more.

Hold the finished pancakes in the heated oven while you repeat the process with the rest of the batter.

QUICK PICKLED RADISHES

WITH CREAM CHEESE ON TOAST

RECOMMENDED BEER
German weissbier
Hills Special Wheat, Yaletown
   Brewing (British Columbia)
Bräu-Weisse, Brauerei Ayinger
   (Germany)

SERVES 4

PREPARATION TIME 20 minutes,
plus 3–6 hours for radishes to pickle

....

1 Tbsp (15 mL) sugar

1 tsp (5 mL) kosher salt

⅔ cup (160 mL) water

⅓ cup (80 mL) white vinegar

small bunch radishes, washed and
leaves removed, sliced thinly

1 package (8 oz/250 g) cream
cheese, softened

½ tsp (2.5 mL) kosher salt

½ tsp (2.5 mL) caraway seeds

freshly ground black pepper

1 Tbsp (15 mL) lemon juice

4 thick pumpernickel rounds

1 Tbsp (15 mL) flat-leaf parsley,
minced

THE FRENCH HAVE an intriguing way of eating radishes. At breakfast time, they spread sliced radishes with soft cultured butter and sprinkle them with flaky salt. The rich, fatty butter stands between the palate and the abrasive radish, and turns what would otherwise be a tear-jerking experience into a pleasant one. The salt helps to brighten all of the flavours.

This recipe is less of a breakfast snack and more of a light lunch or sunny afternoon snack. The salty-sweet quick pickle brine will calm the radishes. The bread adds substance, but it's important that it is only lightly toasted because too-dry bread will dominate and obscure the other textures and besides, pumpernickel burns easily.

Without really planning to, I've created a French version of the English ploughman's lunch. All the elements are here—cheese, bread and a pickled, sharp-flavoured vegetable—and the weissbier completes the picture. Its carbonation will lift fat from the palate and the slight sweetness will tie the bread and cheese together, but most of all the spice notes in the beer will echo those we're adding to the whipped cream cheese.

———— ⫸⫷ ————

Combine the sugar, kosher salt, water and white vinegar in a medium non-reactive bowl. Stir to dissolve the solids—the brine may be a bit cloudy, but there should be no visible salt or sugar at the bottom. Add the sliced radishes. Cover and refrigerate for at least 3 to 6 hours.

In a food processor, combine the cream cheese, kosher salt, caraway seeds, three or four grinds of black pepper, and lemon juice. Process until the ingredients are well mixed and the cheese is noticeably lighter, about 2 to 3 minutes. These ingredients can be combined in a medium mixing bowl and whipped with a hand

mixer, but it will be difficult to introduce as much air as a food processor can.

Very lightly toast the pumpernickel bread. Spread each round generously with cream cheese and top with a layer of pickled radishes. Sprinkle minced parsley on top to garnish.

NOTE The radishes can be pickled a day ahead. If you want to make them further in advance, slice them more thickly so that they retain some crunch.

HOP SHOOTS

WITH WARM BURRATA AND PROSCIUTTO

RECOMMENDED BEER
Kölsch

Arctic Ale, Swans Brewery (British Columbia)

Golden Goddess, Goose Island Beer (Anheuser-Busch) (United States)

SERVES 4–6

PREPARATION TIME 15 minutes

....

1 bunch hop shoots (a good handful)

1 ball burrata (about 1 lb/500 g)

4 thin slices of good-quality prosciutto di Parma (or other aged, dry-cured ham)

¼ cup (60 mL) peppery extra-virgin olive oil

2 Tbsp (30 mL) lemon juice

large pinch flaky sea salt

freshly ground black pepper

lightly toasted bread for serving

HOP SHOOTS WERE eaten as a first springtime green even before the cones were used as a bittering and preservative agent in beer. They are best picked very early in the season when only a few inches tall and bearing a resemblance to tiny asparagus. Side shoots that grow off the main stems later in the season are also edible, but are only tender if picked when very small; otherwise, they need to be blanched in boiling water.

As discussed in the recipe for Pickled Hop Shoots (page 171), you will have this ingredient in abundance if you grow your own hops (or know someone who does). If you don't, it's not really worth trying to buy them.

The trend toward baking cheese is nice because it means fewer occasions when the choice is either fridge-cold cheese or no cheese at all. The problem is that it's easy to overdo it in the hot oven when the hectic preparations for a dinner party set in. Burrata (an Italian cheese made with mozzarella and cream) should be August-afternoon room temperature, and the easiest way to get it there is with a five-minute soak in a bowl of warm water.

Serve with a rustic, crusty country-style bread.

———— ❧ ————

In a large pot of boiling, salted water, blanch the hop shoots for 1 to 2 minutes. Remove and drain thoroughly. (If the shoots are very young and tender, or if you don't mind a little extra chewing, this step is optional.)

Fill a bowl with warm tap water. It should be near the top of the range for what you'd expect from a hot bath. Put the burrata, in its packaging, into the bowl of hot water and let it stand for 5 minutes. Remove from the water, discard the packaging and set the cheese on a serving platter.

Lay the slices of prosciutto on top of each other and roll the pile up like a cigar. With a sharp chef's knife, cut the prosciutto into ¼-inch (.5 cm) strips. In a mixing bowl, combine the shoots, prosciutto, olive oil and lemon juice. Add salt and black pepper to taste and toss thoroughly to combine.

Top heated burrata with prosciutto and hop shoots and another drizzle of best-quality olive oil.

SESAME GINGER
Edamame

RECOMMENDED BEER
Stout
La Bête Noir, Microbrasserie À La
    Fût (Quebec)
Brooklyn Black Chocolate Stout,
    Brooklyn Brewery (United States)

SERVES 4

PREPARATION TIME 25 minutes

COOKING TIME 15 minutes

1 lb (500 g) shell-on, frozen
edamame (or fresh in season)

1½ Tbsp (22.5 mL) white sesame
seeds

½ tsp (2.5 mL) toasted sesame oil

1 tsp (5 mL) peanut or other
neutral oil

1 garlic clove, minced

¾-inch (2 cm) piece ginger, peeled
and grated

½ cup (125 mL) stout

1 tsp (5 mL) honey

1 tsp (5 mL) soy sauce

kosher salt to taste

EDAMAME HAVE GONE from exotic appetizer in fancy sushi restaurants to just about every grocery store freezer case in the last five years or so. They are just soybeans picked early in the summer, at the green stage.

They do come in bags without their shells, but I think it's more fun to serve edamame still in the shell and let guests pop them out themselves. For the most part, the flavour from the marinade stays on the outside, so the trick to getting the whole experience is to put the whole bean in your mouth and pull the shell out while keeping the beans behind your bottom front teeth.

———— ❧ ————

Bring a medium to large pot of salted water to a boil over high heat. Cook the soybeans for 4 minutes. Remove the beans from the boiling water and drain in a colander. Fresh soybeans might take longer to cook than frozen beans, which are either partially or totally cooked before they are packaged. Or if fresh soybeans are particularly young, they might take a bit less. The point is that with fresh beans, you'll need to be vigilant and start tasting around the 3-minute mark.

Toast the sesame seeds in a dry, medium skillet over medium heat until fragrant and beginning to pop. Remove the seeds to a large mixing bowl.

In the same skillet, heat the sesame oil and peanut oil over medium heat for 2 minutes. Add the garlic and ginger and cook, stirring often, for 30 seconds. Pour the beer in, bring to a simmer, and cook until reduced by half. Stir in the honey and soy sauce. Pour the sauce into the same bowl as the sesame seeds.

Add the boiled edamame to the bowl. Toss and taste for seasoning, and add a pinch of kosher salt if necessary.

NO-KNEAD

SOFT PRETZELS

RECOMMENDED BEER
Bock
Maibock, Lighthouse Brewing
   (British Columbia)
Doppelbock Dunkel, Andechser
   Klosterbrauerei (Germany)

MAKES 12 medium pretzels

PREPARATION TIME 20–25
minutes (plus first rising time of
12–18 hours and second rising time
of 15 minutes)

COOKING AND BAKING TIME
30–35 minutes

....

scant ⅔ cup (160 mL) water

scant ⅔ cup (160 mL) bock beer

15 oz (450 g) bread flour
(about 3½ cups/875 mL)

1 tsp (5 mL) table salt

1 tsp (5 mL) instant yeast

FINAL STAGE

6 cups (1.5 L) water

1 Tbsp (15 mL) sugar

scant ¼ cup (60 mL) baking soda

coarse sea salt

PRETZELS ARE THE unofficial bread of southern Germany, and their companionship with beer really needs no explanation.

If you're concerned about appearances, your goal should be to create three holes that are all the same size. The shape won't really affect the taste, but I didn't write the rules.

Some Germans in some parts of Germany prefer their pretzels dipped in melted butter. I fall more into the North American camp and prefer mine dipped in whole-grain mustard. Try them both.

Because pretzel dough needs to be handled more than bread dough during the shaping process, it can't be as wet and sticky as the dough produced by most no-knead recipes. Without that extra moisture the yeast will need some help in developing the necessary gluten, and that means a bit of manipulation. I guess this is more of a low-knead pretzel recipe, but that doesn't have the same ring to it, now does it?

———————— ✦✦✦ ————————

In a small saucepan, set the first amount of water and the beer over low heat and bring to between 90°F and 95°F (32°C and 35°C) (since that's slightly lower than body temperature, it should feel very slightly cool if you dip your finger in).

In a large bowl, with a wooden spoon, mix together the flour (all-purpose is an acceptable substitute for bread flour), salt and yeast. Add the warm water and beer to the flour mixture and stir until the dough forms a shaggy mass. Leaving the dough ball in the bowl, use your hand to knead it for a minute or so. Cover the bowl with plastic wrap and leave to rise for between 12 and 18 hours or until doubled in size.

When you're ready to shape the pretzels, turn the dough out onto a counter and manipulate it into a rough log shape. Divide this into 12 equal portions and cover them with the plastic wrap from the bowl.

METHOD CONTINUES . . .

Heat your oven to 450°F (230°C); set the racks in the middle two positions. Line two cookie sheets with parchment paper or silicone mats.

For the stretching and shaping process, it will help if the dough and counter stick to each other slightly. You may want to lightly flour your hands and the work surface if you have trouble with too much sticking. Roll each piece into a long snake that is at least a foot (30 cm) in length and wider in the middle than at the ends (as if a mouse were only halfway down). For descriptive purposes, let's call one end "Larry" and the other "Randy." Form the piece of dough into a "U" shape and then cross Randy over Larry. Now cross Larry over Randy, making a second twist in the pretzel and then bring both Randy and Larry back to the "belly" of the pretzel and press them in to seal the joint. Move this pretzel to one of the cookie sheets and cover with a kitchen towel. Repeat with the other 11 pieces of dough. Let the pretzels have a full 15 minutes to go through a second rise.

While the pretzels are resting, set your widest sauté pan over medium-high heat and pour in the water. Once it has come to a bare simmer, pour in the sugar and baking soda.

Working in batches, move the pretzels to the hot water bath. I find it's best to start them top-side down for 45 seconds, flip them over for 15 seconds and then use a wide, slotted spoon to move them back to the lined cookie sheet with the top side up. Sprinkle each with a pinch of coarse salt (if the salt doesn't want to stick, brush the tops of the pretzels with a small dose of the baking soda–laced water). Move the cookie sheets to the hot oven and try to offset their position so that the top sheet covers the bottom sheet as little as possible.

Bake for 15 to 17 minutes or until the pretzels turn dark brown. Let the pans cool for 2 minutes and then move the pretzels to a wire rack for another hour. Like most baked breads, pretzels taste great hot and even better if you can manage to let them cool down a bit.

NOTE The water bath gelatinizes the surface starch on the dough, and that gel bakes into a hard, crispy brown crust in the hot oven. Commercial pretzel-making operations use food-grade lye (sodium hydroxide) to raise the pH of the pretzel's pre-bake bath water. Lye is very caustic to utensils, kitchen surfaces and skin, but if recreating the factory recipe is your thing, go ahead and track some down (make sure it's food grade) and use it in the ratio of 1 ounce per quart (30 g per litre) of water and with extreme caution. Frankly, I don't see the point. I've tasted pretzels made with lye and with baking soda (sodium bicarbonate) and can't tell the difference. If you think you can, let me know and we'll arrange a blind taste test.

Bavarians typically decorate their pretzels with a special pretzel salt, made by compressing and screening rock salt. Coarse sea salt is much easier to find and I've liked the results. If you don't have coarse sea salt, it's important to use the largest-grain kosher salt you can find; finer salt will melt into the pretzels and you'll get light-coloured, salty blotches instead of sharp hits of a salty crunch.

RECOMMENDED BEER

Bière de garde

Barrel-Aged Bière de Garde,
  Bellwoods Brewery (Ontario)

Bière de Beloeil, Brasserie Dupont
  (Belgium)

SERVES 4–6

PREPARATION TIME 5 minutes

COOKING TIME 15 minutes

....

FONDUE SAUCE

7½ oz (230 g) shredded Gruyère
(about 2 cups/500 mL)

4 oz (125 g) shredded aged cheddar
(about 1 cup/250 mL)

1 Tbsp (15 mL) cornstarch

2 garlic cloves, finely minced

1 cup (250 mL) bière de garde

1 Tbsp (15 mL) whole-grain mustard

1 Tbsp (15 mL) cider vinegar

2 tsp (10 mL) brandy

freshly ground black pepper

FONDUE IS A classic recipe that came to North American popularity in the 1970s during the heyday of the "easy entertaining" parties. Its deeper roots extend to Switzerland where the liquid and lifting alcohol are more likely to come from white wine. In the German version, various wursts joined cubes of bread in the dipping line. Vegetables are limited, so it's best to serve a green salad beforehand.

Pickles are often mentioned half-heartedly as an afterthought garnish, but I don't see why that should be the case. Cornichons, pickled onions and pickled carrots would all make excellent accompaniments to fondue, and if the fancy strikes, why not spear them and dip them in the cheese?

FONDUE SAUCE Toss the two cheeses and cornstarch together in a medium mixing bowl.

Set a fondue pot over medium heat and add the garlic cloves and beer. When the beer barely simmers, add the cheese, a handful at a time, and stir to melt before adding the next handful. When the cheese sauce is smooth and creamy, add the mustard, vinegar and brandy. Season with a few grinds of black pepper.

1 loaf sourdough bread, cut into 1-inch (2.5 cm) cubes, toasted

¾ lb (375 g) small red-skinned potatoes, halved and boiled till just tender

1 lb (500 g) bratwurst or other mild sausage, poached and cut into 1-inch (2.5 cm) pieces

various pickles

FOR DIPPING Move the fondue pot to its tabletop setup and serve with the bread cubes, potatoes, sausages and pickles.

NOTE Provide long forks for dipping and warn diners that the cheese and especially the fondue pot will be hot. Also, make sure that the fondue setup is secure and can't be knocked over.

WELSH RABBIT

RECOMMENDED BEER

English brown ale

Iron Bridge Brown Ale, Prince
   Edward Island Brewing (PEI)

Newcastle Brown Ale, John Smiths
   (Heineken) (United Kingdom)

SERVES 6

PREPARATION TIME 10 minutes

COOKING TIME 25 minutes

....

1 container (2 good handfuls) cherry
or other small tomatoes, halved.

1 Tbsp (15 mL) olive oil

2 Tbsp (30 mL) unsalted butter

½ yellow cooking onion,
finely minced

½ Tbsp (7.5 mL) flour

1 cup (250 mL) English brown ale

½ tsp (2.5 mL) dry mustard powder

14 oz (400 g) shredded old cheddar
cheese (about 2 cups/500 mL)

1 tsp (5 mL) Worcestershire sauce

pinch cayenne

kosher salt

freshly ground black pepper

½ loaf sourdough bread, crusts
removed, sliced thinly into triangles

BEER AND CHEESE have a natural affinity. While beers have the flavours we associate with grain (malty, bready and biscuit-like) all cut by bitterness, cheese has those we link with milk (lactic, buttery and creamy) enhanced by salt. They also share a cultural history as early manufactured foodstuffs that were created to store the nutrients of perishable wheat and milk.

Many historical accounts of this dish place it as a communal, fireside meal, with cheese sauce bubbling away in a cast iron pot on the hearth while everyone toasted triangles of bread on long forks. I think we can enjoy the same camaraderie by heaping toast points into a large cast iron pan and serving the dish like a plate of nachos.

———— ⟫❦⟪ ————

Position an oven rack in the slot two down from your broiler. Set the broiler to high.

In a 10- to 12-inch (25 to 30 cm) cast iron pan, toss the halved tomatoes with the olive oil until coated. Season with a pinch of kosher salt and a couple of grinds of black pepper. When the broiler is hot, place the pan under it and cook until the tomatoes have just started to blister and take on colour, about 3 to 5 minutes. Transfer the cooked tomatoes to a small bowl, but keep the cast iron pan handy.

In a small saucepan, melt the butter over medium-low heat on your stove's gentlest burner. When most of the moisture has been driven out of the butter and it stops foaming, add the minced onion and cook, stirring frequently, for 5 to 7 minutes or until the onion has softened and just barely starts to turn golden.

When the onion is cooked, shake the flour over top and stir to coat. Cook for 2 minutes to cook out the flour's cereal flavour. With a whisk in one hand, pour the beer into the pan with the other hand

and stir constantly to avoid lumps. Watch the beer closely; it may foam vigorously and the pan should be lifted off the hot burner to avoid a boil-over. Once the beer has foamed and is simmering gently, reduce the heat to low. Stir in the dry mustard and then add the cheese a handful at a time, melting and incorporating each dose before adding the next. Stir in the Worcestershire sauce and cayenne and taste the cheese sauce for seasoning. It will probably need a few grinds of black pepper and possibly a pinch of kosher salt.

Reheat the broiler. Arrange the bread triangles in the cast iron pan with the cooked tomatoes spread throughout. Drizzle the melted cheese sauce over top and place the pan under the hot broiler for 2 to 3 minutes or until the cheese is brown and bubbly.

Serve straight from the pan—on a trivet with a towel wrapped around the handle to protect table and hands.

CHICKEN LIVER
PÂTÉ

RECOMMENDED BEER
English-style barley wine
St-Ambroise Vintage Ale, Brasserie
  McAuslan (Quebec)

SERVES 8–10

PREPARATION TIME 10 minutes

COOKING TIME 15 minutes, plus
at least 1–2 hours to cool

....

1 lb (500 g) chicken livers

3 Tbsp (45 mL) unsalted butter

1 shallot, finely minced

1 branch thyme, leaves removed
from stems and minced

3 Tbsp (45 mL) plus 1 Tbsp (15 mL)
barley wine

½ tsp (2.5 mL) freshly
grated nutmeg

¼ tsp (1 mL) freshly ground
white pepper

4 tsp (20 mL) olive oil

1 tsp (5 mL) kosher salt

THERE ARE TWO ways to make this classic French appetizer. Either sauté the livers and aromatic vegetables and then blend them with the dairy, or blend everything first and cook slowly in a moderate oven. It's hard to say that one way is right and the other wrong because authorities as respected as *Gourmet Magazine,* David Chang and Julia Child are divided—fairly evenly—between the two. I like the cook-first solution because it's faster and only requires careful attention for a short, critical period.

The strong barley wine stands in for the more traditional brandy or vermouth. It brings the flavour-carrying power of its high alcohol content but matches better with the warm spices than the fortified wine usually does. American barley wines are noticeably hoppier than their across-the-pond cousins and the bitterness will really concentrate during the deglazing step, so it's important to use an English-style barley wine that is relatively low in bitterness.

———— ⁂ ————

Use a sharp paring knife to clean the livers of any membranes, nodes of fat or generally any bits that don't look like dark, reddish-brown liver.

Set a pan over medium heat and melt the butter. When foaming subsides add the minced shallot to the pan and stir to coat with butter. Cook until the shallot becomes translucent and softens, about 4 minutes. Add pieces of liver and minced thyme and toss to coat in hot butter. Cook for 3 minutes and then flip all of the pieces of liver. After another 2 minutes start removing the smallest pieces. Larger ones may need an extra minute or two. The liver should still have a pink blush on the inside.

Pour 3 tablespoons (45 mL) of the barley wine into the pan and scrape the bottom to deglaze.

Transfer the cooked liver and shallot mixture to a food processor fitted with the slicing blade. Add the nutmeg and white pepper. Process on high speed until a smooth paste forms. While the processor is running, pour in the additional barley wine and the olive oil and salt, and let the processor run until enough air has been integrated into the pâté to make the colour noticeably lighter.

Use a spatula to transfer the pâté to a serving dish, cover tightly and refrigerate. Serve with lightly toasted baguette rounds.

SALADS AND SOUPS

Recipes in this section can be served as a first course or perhaps two combined to make a light meal. Especially on hot summer days—when beer is the first drink we reach for—salads that can be made in advance will come in handy. The two soups demonstrate how well craft beer contributes to the flavour and aroma of a dish when it's used as part of the liquid base.

TABBOULEH

RECOMMENDED BEER

Belgian witbier

Belgian Wit, Mill Street Brewery
   (Ontario)

Fantôme Blanche, Brasserie
   Fantôme (Belgium)

SERVES 4

PREPARATION TIME 15 minutes,
plus 1–2 hours for bulgar to soak

....

½ cup (125 mL) medium-ground
bulgar

¼ cup (60 mL) Belgian witbier

4 small plum tomatoes (or 3
medium), halved, seeded and diced

½ English cucumber, peeled and
chopped into medium dice

2 Tbsp (30 mL) lemon juice, freshly
squeezed

6 Tbsp (90 mL) extra-virgin olive oil

¼ tsp (1 mL) cayenne pepper

½ bunch flat-leaf parsley, chopped

8–10 leaves mint, stacked, rolled
and chopped into fine shreds

½ small red onion, finely minced

kosher salt

freshly ground black pepper

TABBOULEH IS THE muscle for the gang of no-cook salads that can be prepared at the height of summer without heating an already stifling kitchen. Bulgar is whole-grain wheat (or nearly so, with a bit of the bran usually removed) that has been coarsely ground and parboiled. The parboiling means that for cold salads like tabbouleh, bulgar only needs to be soaked to make it edible.

Most recipes use water to soak bulgar, but if we choose a beer with flavours that match well with wheat, herbs and a lemony vinaigrette, this is a great opportunity to add flavour. With coriander and orange peel, a Belgian witbier (a wheat beer whose name comes from the Dutch for "white beer") seems like the ideal candidate.

We don't want the tomatoes to make the salad soggy, so I have chosen plum tomatoes for their high flesh-to-moisture ratio. Dig the seeds and watery jelly out from inside the tomatoes using a large soup spoon.

Follow the instructions on the bulgar package for presoaking, but substitute beer for water. Leave some extra time as leeway because some brands of bulgar take longer to soften than the package specifies.

Mix the soaked bulgar with plum tomatoes, cucumber, lemon juice, olive oil, cayenne pepper, parsley, mint and red onion. Season with a large pinch of salt and a few grinds of black pepper. Taste and adjust salt, pepper and lemon juice if necessary.

WILTED DANDELION SALAD

WITH BACON VINAIGRETTE

RECOMMENDED BEER
German weissbier
Hefe-Weissbier, Muskoka Brewery
   (Ontario)
Hefe Weissbier, Weihenstephaner
   (Germany)

SERVES 4

PREPARATION TIME 20 minutes

....

3 slices thick-cut bacon

1 bunch dandelion leaves, washed

4 medium (or 6 small) radishes, thinly sliced

fine sea salt

1 shallot, finely minced

1 Tbsp (15 mL) Beer Vinegar (pages 167–170), or sherry vinegar or malt vinegar

½ tsp (2.5 mL) Dijon mustard

IN THE SPRING, especially where lawn pesticides have been banned, dandelions cover our lawns. Luckily, what can be a frustration to a meticulous homeowner is an edible delight to the home cook. They have also gained in popularity to the point where many supermarkets now carry bunches of the cultivated leaves.

If you do pick your own, take only the small tender leaves, preferably from plants that haven't flowered. Make sure your dandelions are growing in a space that hasn't been sprayed, and wash them well to remove grit. Arugula is an acceptable substitute.

There are three recipes in this book for making your own vinegar from beer. The dressing for a strongly flavoured salad is a great opportunity to use the product of those experiments, but if yours isn't ready yet feel free to substitute sherry vinegar or store-bought malt vinegar.

———— >»·«< ————

Heat a pan (preferably cast iron) over medium heat. Cut the bacon into large postage-stamp rectangles and spread them over the bottom of the hot pan. Reduce the heat to low and fry the bacon until barely crisp. After somewhere between 10 and 12 minutes the bacon will start to sizzle less and colour on the bottom. This means that most of the water has evaporated from the pan and that the bacon should be flipped and watched more closely. Bacon can be fried more quickly, but low heat will cook it more evenly.

Tear any large dandelion leaves into manageable pieces. Place the leaves and sliced radishes in a bowl. Season lightly with the fine sea salt.

When the bacon is brown all over and barely crisp, remove to a paper towel–lined plate. Tip the pan to one side and evaluate how much fat is left in the bottom. If it looks like more than about 2 tablespoons (30 mL), pour the extra off. Increase the heat to medium and dump the minced shallot into the pan. Cook, stirring often with a whisk, until the shallot has softened and become translucent, but only barely coloured, about 2 minutes. Add the vinegar and mustard to the pan and whisk vigorously until combined. Pour the warm vinaigrette over the salad and top with the bacon.

Warm Potato Salad

WITH SUMMER SAUSAGE

RECOMMENDED BEER
Pilsner
Red Canoe Lager, Canoe Brewing
  (British Columbia)
Prima Pils, Victory Brewing (United
  States)

SERVES 4–6

PREPARATION TIME 10 minutes,
plus 30 minutes for vinegar to blend

COOKING TIME 20 minutes

....

3–4 Yukon Gold potatoes, each cut
into 4–6 chunks

2 medium sweet potatoes, peeled
and each cut into 10–12 chunks

3 Tbsp (45 mL) Beer Vinegar
(pages 167–170) or cider vinegar

4 oz (125 g) summer sausage, cut
into small chunks

4 small radishes, sliced

2 ribs celery, sliced

2 scallions, tough part of the greens
discarded, the rest thinly sliced

2 large dill pickles, finely chopped

½ cup (125 mL) olive oil

1 Tbsp (15 mL) whole-grain mustard

TWO TYPES OF potatoes for colour and flavour contrast, a vinegar dressing and summer sausage: this salad is miles away from the gloppy, mayo-drenched versions that have plagued church picnics and potlucks since the beginning of time.

The number-one key to delicious potato salad, shared first with me by Alton Brown on an episode of *Good Eats,* is that the potatoes need to be introduced to the vinegar while they're still hot. This applies whether you plan to serve your salad warm, room temperature or refrigerator cold. (And depending on what else is on the menu and where the mercury sits, there is a time and place for all three.) By some culinary alchemy, the hot potatoes take on the earthy flavours from the vinegar, which contrasts beautifully with the fattier dressing.

My preference order for what acid you use here runs from homemade malt vinegar to cider vinegar, to rice wine vinegar. Potatoes are a blank canvas for the flavour of vinegar, so this is a great salad to showcase your homemade beer vinegar.

Bring a large pot of salted water to a boil. Drop in the chunks of Yukon Gold potatoes. After 2 minutes add the sweet potatoes and cook until all the chunks are tender enough that the point of a sharp knife meets only slight resistance. Drain in a colander and let cool for a minute. Transfer potato chunks to a large non-reactive serving bowl and pour vinegar over top. Toss to coat, cover with plastic wrap and let stand for at least 30 minutes.

Add the sausage, radishes, celery, scallions and chopped dill pickles to the potatoes. Shake the olive oil and mustard together in a small Mason jar and pour over the salad. Toss to coat.

NOTE Summer sausage is so called because it is preserved in a way that lets it be stored at room temperature. Curing salt and a low pH make traditional versions shelf stable and also lend that characteristic acidic twang that works so nicely with potatoes. Summer sausage does not need to be cooked. It's best to look for a large chunk (have one cut for you at the deli counter) that can be cut into smaller pieces the size of very small croutons.

smoked salmon,

POTATOES AND GREEN BEANS

RECOMMENDED BEER
Saison
Nickel Brook Le Paysan Saison,
 Better Bitters Brewing (Ontario)
Fantôme Saison, Brasserie Fantôme
 (Belgium)

SERVES 4

PREPARATION TIME 10 minutes

COOKING TIME 15–20 minutes

....

½ lb (250 g) fresh green beans,
washed and ends trimmed

1 lb (500 g) fingerling potatoes,
washed and halved

6 slices cold-smoked salmon

⅔ cup (160 mL) extra-virgin olive oil

¼ cup (60 mL) lemon juice

1½ Tbsp (22.5 mL) chopped dill
fronds

kosher salt

freshly ground black pepper

4½ oz (140 g) goat cheese,
crumbled (about ¼ cup/60 mL)

LIKE MANY OTHER agricultural products, potatoes have been made into an all-season crop. That's convenient, but this salad is at its best when made from the first knobby specimens that start to show up in farmers' markets (or your garden) in early summer.

I like the way the smoked salmon's pungent saltiness is amplified by the heat from the potatoes and green beans. The bold flavours of grassy green beans, earthy potatoes and salty-smoky salmon are complemented nicely by the spice and zest flavours in saison. Salads like this that are based on peak-of-summer produce need to be served with a beverage that can stand some chilling, and there again saison fits the bill.

———— ⊰≫⧓⧏≪⊱ ————

Bring a large pot of salted water to a rolling boil. Immerse green beans in the water and cook for 2 minutes. Use tongs or a spider skimmer to transfer the green beans from the water into a strainer. Shake as much water as possible from the beans and spread them out on a large cookie sheet to cool.

Cook the potatoes in the same pot of salted water until they yield to the point of a thin-bladed knife. Start checking after 9 or 10 minutes.

While the potatoes are cooking, lay the slices of smoked salmon in a pile, roll them up like a cigar and slice into thin strips.

Combine the olive oil, lemon juice, dill, a pinch of kosher salt and two grinds of black pepper in a small Mason jar. Shake vigorously to emulsify.

Toss potatoes, green beans, smoked salmon and goat cheese together in a large mixing bowl and season with a generous pinch of kosher salt. Pour the dressing over top and stir to coat. Serve on separate plates or let guests serve themselves from a communal platter.

FRENCH ONION

SOUP

RECOMMENDED BEER
Bock
Deviator Doppelbock, Cameron's
Brewing (Ontario)
Celebrator Doppelbock, Brauerei
Ayinger (Germany)

SERVES 4

PREPARATION TIME 30 minutes

COOKING TIME 1 hour

....

4 lb (1.8 kg) yellow cooking onions

3 Tbsp (45 mL) unsalted butter

1 Tbsp (15 mL) sugar

½ tsp (2.5 mL) plus a pinch baking
soda

4 cups (1 L) water

2 cups (500 mL) bock

3⅔ cups (900 mL) reduced-sodium
beef broth

bouquet garni (1 bay leaf, 4–5 sprigs
thyme, 4–5 sprigs flat-leaf parsley
tied into a cheesecloth package)

1 tsp (5 mL) kosher salt

freshly ground black pepper

4 slices sourdough bread, trimmed
to fit broiler-safe ramekins or
French onion soup bowls

4 oz (125 g) shredded Gruyère
(about ¾ cup/185 mL)

THE FOUR-WAY friendship between beer, cheese, bread and onions is a thread that runs through more than a couple of recipes in this book. If chosen with a bit of care, these four elements emphasize each other's strong points and cover the weak ones. They sing in harmony.

Onion soup is one of the easiest (and cheapest) dishes to make. Traditional recipes demand an extended servitude to stove-side stirring, but really with a bit of science this isn't necessary. The key to getting the most flavour from the onions is to carefully walk the narrow line between very dark golden brown and burnt. Raising the pH by adding a bit of baking soda to the pot will stretch that line wider.

Other than a sharp knife, a straight-edged wooden spoon is probably the most useful kitchen tool that you can hold in your hand. I'm hard pressed to imagine making this recipe without one. They cost only a few dollars and every kitchen should have one.

———————— ⟫⟫⟪⟪ ————————

Onions have a root end and a top end. Cut a thick slice off the top end and then bisect the onions through the poles. This approach will make it easier to peel the skin away, and leaving the root end mostly intact will make the onions easier to handle while cutting them. After peeling, cut the onions in thin slices that preserve the grain (cuts will run from root to tip, not across). Stack the half moons and cut down through the middle of each pile.

Melt the butter in a heavy stockpot or enamelled Dutch oven set over medium-high heat. When the foaming subsides, add the onions, sugar, baking soda and a pinch of salt and stir to coat evenly. Measure out the water and have it near at hand while stirring the onions. Each time the browned bits coating the pan threaten to burn, add about a ½ cup (125 mL) of water, scrape vigorously and stir thoroughly. Use a sort of pancake-flipping motion that will move the onions at the top of the pile to the bottom and vice versa. After about 20 minutes the onions should be very soft and deeply caramelized.

After the fourth addition of water has evaporated, add the beer and scrape and stir again. Immediately add the beef broth, remaining water and bouquet garni. Bring the soup to a simmer, cover and reduce heat to low for 30 minutes.

Heat your oven's broiler to high and set a rack in the second-highest position. Place the slices of bread on the rack under the broiler and toast until golden-brown on the top side. This will only take a couple of minutes, so watch carefully that the bread doesn't burn.

Remove the herbs from the pot and stir in the salt and a couple of grinds of black pepper. Taste the soup and add more salt if necessary. (Different brands of broth have drastically different salt contents, so it's important to taste.)

Place your ramekins or bowls on a cookie sheet and fill each bowl with soup to about an inch (2.5 cm) from the top. Each bowl gets a piece of bread (toasted side down) and a quarter of the grated cheese. Move the cookie sheet into the oven and broil until the cheese is bubbling and has started to brown. Like toasting the bread, this will happen quickly, so pay careful attention.

NOTE I'm an inveterate substituter and I understand that with many of these recipes, you will make substitutions too. But please don't use red onions here. They will colour the soup an odd, unappetizing blue instead of the deep, rich shade of brown that we're after. This has to do with the way the onion's colour pigment reacts to heat and cellular breakdown. If you have homemade chicken broth, you can substitute 2 cups (500 mL) of it for the water that is added with the beef broth and bouquet garni, but be sure to reduce the salt you add at the end of the recipe to compensate for any salt in the chicken broth.

NEW ENGLAND
Clam Chowder

RECOMMENDED BEER
German weissbier
Beachcomber Summer Ale,
   Vancouver Island Brewery
   (British Columbia)
Hefe-Weissbier, Paulaner
   (Germany)

SERVES 4–6

PREPARATION TIME 30 minutes

COOKING TIME 30 minutes

....

3 lb (1.5 kg) clams (cherrystone or
other medium-large types)

1 cup (250 mL) clam juice

1½ cups (375 mL) weissbier

7 oz (200 g) bacon, cut into small
chunks

2 Tbsp (30 mL) unsalted butter

1 yellow cooking onion, finely diced

3 cups (750 mL) milk

2 lbs (1 kg) Yukon Gold potatoes,
peeled and cut into ½-inch (1 cm)
chunks

3 sprigs of thyme, tied in a bundle
with kitchen twine

1 bay leaf

1 cup (250 mL) heavy cream

kosher salt

freshly ground black pepper

oyster crackers for serving

THE NEW ENGLAND vs. Manhattan debate is really just window dressing because I think it's a stretch to call the tomato-based version a chowder. Based on a bit of cream and thickened with potatoes, the New England version is hearty and full of rich clam flavours. Serve with oyster crackers and plenty of weissbier.

Tap any open clams against a hard surface and discard the ones whose shells don't close. Move the clams to a large bowl and cover with cold water. Let stand for an hour until the clams have ejected any sandy grit into the water. Lift each clam out of the water and scrub grit from the outside of the shell under cold running water. Place the cleaned clams in a large bowl.

Set a large Dutch oven or heavy-bottomed stockpot over medium heat and pour in the clam juice and ½ cup (125 mL) of the beer. Cover the pot. Once the liquid is simmering and has filled the pot with steam, dump the clams into the pot and replace the lid. Have a large bowl standing by. After about 4 minutes lift the lid and move any clams that have opened to the bowl. Replace the lid and check again every minute or two. Any clams that have not opened after 9 or 10 minutes should be discarded.

Pour the liquid in the bottom of the Dutch oven through a large, fine-mesh sieve set over a large measuring cup. Do the same with any liquid that collects in the bottom of the clam bowl. Clean the sieve.

Return the Dutch oven to the stove over medium heat. Fry the bacon chunks until they have rendered several large spoonfuls of fat and have started to turn brown, about 6 minutes or so. Add the butter and onion to the pot and stir to coat the onion pieces with the bacon fat. Once the onion has softened and become translucent, about 6 minutes, add the rest of the beer, milk, potatoes, bundle of thyme, bay leaf and cooking juices that were collected in the measuring cup.

When the chowder begins to bubble, reduce heat to medium-low and simmer uncovered, stirring occasionally, until the potatoes are very tender, 12 to 14 minutes.

While the chowder is simmering, remove the clam meat to a cutting board and discard the shells. Chop the clam meat roughly and set aside in a medium bowl. Use a wide slotted spoon to lift the solids out of the Dutch oven and put them into the bowl with the clam meat, discarding the thyme bundle and bay leaf.

Use an immersion blender to thoroughly blend the liquid in the Dutch oven. Return the solids to the pot and stir in the cream. Bring to a simmer. Carefully taste the chowder. It will probably need a heavy pinch of kosher salt and a few grinds of black pepper.

Serve very warm with oyster crackers on the side.

NOTE Like mussels, clams are alive until you cook them. That means that they need to be stored in a way that lets them breathe. An open container in the bottom, back corner of your refrigerator is best.

NICOLE BARRY

CEO, Half Pints Brewing Company
Winnipeg, Manitoba

NICOLE BARRY, THE CEO of Half Pints Brewing Company, stands at the helm of a small ship in a very small body of water. The company that she started with her business partner and brewmaster, David Rudge, is Manitoba's only locally owned craft brewery.

As a long-time craft beer lover, Barry appreciates the freedom that a smaller market has given her. Half Pints has grown in small, manageable steps and turned down the opportunity to work with venture capital. By doing this, the company has avoided the need to grow quickly by producing a mass-market beer.

Before starting the brewery, Barry received a Bachelor of Business Administration from the Southern Alberta Institute of Technology. She also earned her Certified General Accountant designation and worked in the insurance industry as part of her and Rudge's plan to open a brewery by their early thirties.

As the CEO of her small business, she applies that accounting training on a near-daily basis. When I talked to her she was careful to explain that one of her goals is to teach the brewers how to buy ingredients efficiently, but definitely not to direct them what to buy. She wants every product in the Half Pints range to taste like beer made by brewers who are proud of their product.

The selection of beers they make follows the fairly usual three-tier model. Four flagship beers, St. James Pale Ale, Bulldog Amber Ale, Little Scrapper IPA and Stir Stick Stout, are produced in larger quantities and are available regularly. These are complemented by two seasonal offerings (Saison De La Ceinture Fléchée and Le Temps Noir) and a long list of special releases that tend to score highly on the niche beer-rating sites. Favourites of mine include the Humulus Ludicrous double IPA and the Pothole Porter, and I also quite liked their Punk N' Fest pumpkin ale.

A large part of operating as the only locally owned, truly craft brewery in a market is customer education. As Winnipeg's beer drinkers have come to accept the special-release cask ales, a new challenge has presented itself. Instead of trying to get customers to accept full-flavoured beer that isn't served ice-cold, Half Pints now needs to encourage an appreciation for the ephemeral nature of special one-off releases.

As Half Pints continues to expand carefully, they are utilizing the option of exporting to other provinces as a release valve for excess capacity. Barry knows that the larger beer markets in British Columbia, Alberta and Ontario will buy up pretty much whatever she doesn't plan to sell in Manitoba.

As a beer drinker in Ontario, I'm happy to have any opportunity for an expanded selection of delicious craft beer. Appreciating the small scale of operations also means recognizing that they won't always be able to serve a national market.

VEGETABLES

The list of foods that are difficult to pair with wine includes many vegetables. Artichokes, green beans and olives are three good examples. Fried foods like Belgian frîtes and onion rings can overwhelm the subtleties in many wines. With its hoppy bitterness, tart acidity and grease-cutting carbonation, beer can handle all of these with aplomb.

BELGIAN

FRÎTES

RECOMMENDED BEER
Pilsner
Pilsner, Steam Whistle Brewing
   (Ontario)

SERVES 4–6

PREPARATION TIME 30 minutes

COOKING TIME 20–30 minutes

....

1½ lb (750 g) Yukon Gold potatoes

3 cups (750 mL) peanut oil or rice bran oil

fine sea salt

HOMEMADE FRÎTES ARE a great occasional indulgence. There is something about the pleasant effort it takes to make them that makes it feel healthier than eating them in a restaurant to me.

Frîtes are at the core of the canon of Belgian recipes designed to pair well with craft beer. An easy-drinking pilsner with a moderate amount of refreshing hops is the perfect foil for salty, hot frîtes. Put a twist on the Belgian tradition of serving these in a paper cone by adding a generous dollop of Hop Mayonnaise (page 166).

Before it can become a delicious frîte, two things have to happen to a piece of potato: the inside has to cook (water turns to steam, cells break down and starches gelatinize), and the outside has to turn to a crispy golden brown. The problem is that the first process takes time and happens at a low temperature, while the latter needs higher heat for a short duration. The usual solution is a double fry: poach the potatoes in warm oil, remove and drain while the oil heats to a higher temperature, and then flash-fry them to crisp the outside. The even better solution (which I read about first in Jeffrey Steingarten's book *The Man Who Ate Everything*) is to start the potatoes in cold oil and heat the pan slowly so that it passes through the poaching stage before getting to the second, hotter temperature.

———— ❧ ————

Peel the potatoes around their middles, but leave the ends unpeeled for a hint of rusticity. Have a large bowl of cold water standing by. Use a sharp chef's knife to cut the potatoes into long batons about ½ inch (1 cm) around. As you work, move the cut potatoes to the bowl of water, and when they are all cut agitate them in the water to knock off some of the surface starch. Lay out a clean, dry kitchen towel. Remove the potato pieces from the water (letting as much drain away as possible) and spread them out on the towel. Use a second towel to thoroughly pat the potatoes dry.

Place a large Dutch oven or heavy-bottomed stockpot (at least 10 inches/25 cm in diameter) over your stove's largest burner. Distribute the potatoes over the bottom of the pot. Pour the oil over them to barely cover.

Turn the heat to high and monitor the oil's temperature closely with a probe or deep-frying thermometer. Two things will indicate that the frîtes are cooked: the oil will have reached 350°F (175°C) and they will be a dark golden brown. Remove the frîtes to a cookie sheet lined with paper towel. Season generously with fine sea salt.

NOTE Some fried potato enthusiasts (including some Belgians) prefer theirs fried in animal fat, or at least part animal fat. That usually means duck fat, beef drippings or even horse fat. All are interesting experiments, but I find they often just coat my mouth in grease and obscure the potato flavour. I prefer peanut or rice bran oil. If you can't find those, sunflower, vegetable or canola oil are acceptable substitutes.

ONION RINGS

RECOMMENDED BEER
Belgian witbier
Cheval Blanc, Les Brasseurs RJ
(Quebec)
Blanche des Honnelles, Brasserie de
l'Abbaye des Rocs (Belgium)

SERVES 4-6

PREPARATION TIME 15 minutes

COOKING TIME 4-6 minutes per batch

....

5 cups (1.25 L) peanut
or rice bran oil

1 cup (250 mL) witbier, cold

2 oz (60 g) all-purpose flour (about
½ cup/125 mL)

2 oz (60 g) rice flour (about
⅓ cup/80 mL) plus 2 Tbsp (30 mL)
for dusting rings

½ tsp (2.5 mL) baking powder

¼ tsp (1 mL) fine sea salt

1 large red onion, cut into ¾-inch
(2 cm) slices

COMPARED TO FRIES, when hand-dipped and made to order, onion rings are difficult for a restaurant to manage well. I'll be honest that these aren't an everyday recipe for me, but if you're going to indulge, make sure you do it right.

Surrounding hot slices of onion, the banana, orange and clove flavours in the witbier will brighten and concentrate. I use red onion for this recipe because I'm a bit of an oddball. Spanish onions are more traditional and are a good choice if you can't find a big enough (noticeably larger than your fist) red onion.

———— »»»««« ————

Lay out two cookie sheets and place a wire rack on each. This rig will work both for letting excess batter drip away and to cool the rings once they come out of the hot oil.

Set a Dutch oven over medium heat and fill with 2 inches (5 cm) of oil. Heat the oil to 375°F (190°C).

Pour the cold beer into a medium mixing bowl. Use a fine-mesh strainer to sift the flours into the beer. Add baking powder and salt, and mix to combine, but be careful not to overmix. Put slices of onion in a resealable bag or lidded container with the 2 tablespoons (30 mL) of rice flour and shake to coat the onion lightly.

Use tongs or chopsticks to transfer onion pieces from flour to batter and then to the racks set over the cookie sheets, where excess batter can drop off.

Carefully transfer the battered rings to the hot oil and continue to monitor the oil's temperature. Work in batches that are small enough to not crowd the pan. Cook for 2 to 3 minutes a side or until rings are deep golden brown. Hold cooked rings on a clean wire rack while you fry subsequent batches. Season the rings with fine sea salt immediately after they come out of the hot oil.

NOTE For this recipe, the beer should come straight from the fridge. Cold beer is better because cold liquids hold carbonation better and carbonation is what breaks the gluten strands and keeps the crust light and crisp.

SMOKY

COLLARD GREENS

RECOMMENDED BEER
Smoked ale
Charbonnière, Microbrasserie Dieu
   du Ciel! (Quebec)

SERVES 4

PREPARATION TIME 10 minutes

COOKING TIME 20 minutes

....

1 bunch collard greens, washed

3 Tbsp (45 mL) unsalted butter

1 cup (250 mL) smoked ale

2 Tbsp (30 mL) cider vinegar

kosher salt and freshly ground black
pepper to taste

COLLARDS STAND BESIDE the likes of kale and mustard greens in the lineup of heartiest green leafy vegetables. They do need a relatively long time to cook, but like spinach and Brussels sprouts we've finally come to see that an hour of boiling is way too much. Green vegetables usually only need two or three minutes in boiling water to shock their colour and barely tenderize.

The connection between collards and smoked pork (usually bacon or ham hock) is almost sacrosanct. I'm going to take a risk and suggest that a smoked rauchbier could act as a fine stand-in. If you just can't handle the idea of vegetarian collard greens, go ahead and scale the butter back by half and fry three strips of good-quality bacon in it.

———————— ❧ ————————

Lay the collards in a pile. Use a chef's knife to cut out the stems and discard. Roll the pile into a cigar and cut ribbons about half an inch (1 cm) wide.

In a large sauté pan or skillet (for which you have a tight-fitting lid), heat the butter on medium until it foams, the foaming subsides and it just barely starts to colour. Add the cut greens to the pan along with the beer and use a pair of tongs to mix the pan's contents together. Put the lid on and increase the heat to high. Cook for about 10 minutes.

Remove the lid, stir the greens and cook until the beer has almost totally evaporated, about 8 minutes more.

Kill the heat and stir in the vinegar. Season to taste with kosher salt and black pepper.

RAPINI

RECOMMENDED BEER
Doppelbock
Captivator Doppelbock, Tree
    Brewing (British Columbia)
Korbinian, Weihenstephaner
    (Germany)

SERVES 4

PREPARATION TIME
10–15 minutes

COOKING TIME 10 minutes

....

1 bunch rapini (about ¾ lb/375 g),
washed

3 Tbsp (45 mL) olive oil

2 garlic cloves, finely minced

1 pinch red pepper flakes

¼ cup (60 mL) doppelbock

2 tsp (10 mL) freshly squeezed
lemon juice

kosher salt

RAPINI (OR BROCCOLI RABE) just might be my favourite green vegetable. It tastes enough like pure healthiness to cancel the guilt of fried chicken or an entire slab of ribs. The bitterness helps to cut through the fat in heavier meat dishes. The sweet toffee-like notes from the beer will help balance and brighten the rapini's flavour.

After the rapini has been washed and chopped, put it into your widest saucepan that has a lid. If it all fits easily, you can use that pan for both stages. If not, you'll have to use your pasta pot to blanch the rapini and then a wide skillet for the sauté stage.

Serve with Wild Fried Chicken (page 121) or Stout-Braised Lamb Shank (page 114).

———— ⟫⟩⟨⟨ ————

Chop the rapini into 2-inch (5 cm) lengths and discard the woody ends of the stems. Fill a large, very wide saucepan with cold water to the halfway point. Set over high heat, generously salt the water and cover. Have a large colander ready in your sink. When the water comes to a boil, dump in the rapini and cover as best you can. After 1 minute use a pair of tongs to stir the rapini so that the pieces on top are in the water. After 3 more minutes pour the contents of the pan into the colander and let the water drain.

Add the olive oil to the saucepan, reduce the heat to medium-high and heat the oil for 2 minutes. Add the garlic and red pepper flakes and cook for 30 seconds. Dump the well-drained rapini back into the pan and stir to coat. Cook for 2 minutes before pouring in the beer and lemon juice. Cook for another minute or until the beer is noticeably reduced. Season with a big pinch of kosher salt.

CORN ON THE COB

RECOMMENDED BEER
Pilsner
Prison Break Breakout Pilsner,
    Double Trouble Brewing (Ontario)

SERVES 6-8

PREPARATION TIME 10 minutes

COOKING TIME 7-8 minutes

....

1 dozen corn on the cob, shucked

EVEN THROUGH THE printed page I can sense your raised eyebrows and skeptical grunts. *"Beer isn't on the ingredient list,"* *"No worthy craft beers use corn as an ingredient,"* and *"Cooking in a cooler seems like a gimmick,"* I can hear you complain.

During the hottest days of summer, when corn is at the peak of its season, our coolers are usually stocked with crisp lagers and pale ales. The sweet corn and dry, slightly bitter beer are natural partners. Even if this book weren't about beer, I'd include this recipe because cooking corn on the cob like this is convenient and avoids turning your kitchen into even more of a sauna. The hot water cooks the corn, the corn cools the water so that it doesn't overcook, and the cooler holds everything butter-melting hot until you're ready for it.

I hope it goes without saying that your cooler should be absolutely spotless before using it for this recipe. Use hot soapy water and a bit of vinegar (rather than bleach). Pour cold water from your kettle into the cooler to get a sense of how many kettlefuls will be needed to barely cover all of the corn. You'd like for all the water to be boiling at once so it helps to call a second kettle or large pot into service.

After shucking the corn and cleaning the cobs of all their silk, snap off the stalk "handles." The corn won't be so hot that you can't hold it and the stalk ends would get in the way as you arrange the corn in the cooler.

Try to fit all of the corn in one layer at the bottom of the clean beer cooler.

Pour boiling water over the corn and close the lid tightly. Let the cooler sit for 3 minutes, and then reach in with a pair of tongs and spin the cobs so that the other side is exposed to the hot water. The corn will be ready after another 4 to 5 minutes, but can be held for up to 30 minutes.

NOTE Coolers are lined with food-grade plastic and there is very little opportunity for anything to leach from the plastic into the water and then into your food. However, if you are particularly concerned, only use a recently manufactured cooler and remove the corn as soon as it is cooked.

NOODLES _{AND} RICE

The dishes in this section share a common starchy backbone. They might have been called "sides" 20 or 30 years ago when meat was the expected centrepiece for every meal. I think all of them except the beer-steamed rice would stand perfectly well as main dishes. That's usually because they include a delicious, beer-based sauce.

Keep in mind that if your sauce involves reducing beer, it's important to choose one that is not too bitter.

Pasta

RECOMMENDED BEER
English brown ale
Brown Ale, Mill Street Brewery
   (Ontario)
Highgate Dark Mild, Highgate
   (HWBC Ltd.) (United Kingdom)

SERVES 2

PREPARATION TIME 10 minutes

COOKING TIME 15–20 minutes

....

1 Tbsp (15 mL) olive oil

6 oz (175 g) lamb sausages

5 oz (150 g) farfalle (bowtie) pasta

1 Tbsp (15 mL) flour

⅓ cup (80 mL) English brown ale

⅓ cup (80 mL) milk

2 oz (60 g) Gorgonzola or other
creamy blue cheese, crumbled

2 handfuls arugula, washed

freshly ground black pepper

FULL DISCLOSURE: I don't have an Italian grandmother. For all I know, this combination of ingredients may never have been assembled by anyone's *nonna*. That said, both farfalle (Italian for "butterflies") and Gorgonzola share a common home in the northern Italian region of Lombardy. The bowtie pasta does a great job of picking up the creamy, meat-flecked sauce; the peppery arugula fares well against the other earthy, pungent flavours.

We make small (3-inch/8 cm), caseless lamb sausages and freeze them. Seasoned with salt, pepper, fennel, chili flakes and a bit of fresh mint, they are a convenient source for that just-right small hit of meat in a quick weekday dinner. You could just as well buy fresh lamb sausages, ground lamb, or in a pinch even ground beef. Break your sausages out of the case. If you use ground meat, season it with a pinch each of fennel seeds, red pepper flakes, salt and a few grinds of black pepper. For the sauce, whole milk is ideal, but lower-fat versions will also do.

Bring a pot of cold water to a rolling boil over high heat. Season it heavily with coarse salt.

Heat the olive oil in a wide, heavy-bottomed sauté pan over medium heat for 3 minutes. Crumble the sausage meat (or seasoned ground meat) into the hot oil and let it sit until well-browned on one side.

Around this point you should get the pasta started. Follow the package's instructions on cooking time except that you'll transfer the pasta to the sauce for the last minute or so.

Stir the lamb with a straight-edged wooden spoon so that it browns evenly. Reduce heat to medium-low and scatter flour evenly over the meat. Continue stirring for 2 minutes or until the flour has a nutty smell, indicating that its raw flavour has been cooked out. Pour in the ale and scrape the bottom of the pan. Add the milk and reduce the heat to low.

Gradually add the blue cheese, stirring each addition separately to melt before adding the next.

When the pasta is a minute from al dente, use a wide, slotted spoon to move it to the pan with the sauce. The bowties will naturally bring some of the starchy water with them, but judge how much is needed based on how thick the sauce looks. You may need to add another soup spoon or so's worth of water from the pasta pot.

Stir to coat the pasta in cheesy sauce. Add the arugula and a couple of generous grinds of black pepper and stir to combine (the hot pasta will wilt the arugula). Serve immediately.

BaSmati RicE

STEAMED WITH BEER

RECOMMENDED BEER
Lager
Vienna Lager, King Brewery
(Ontario)
Pilsner, Weihenstephaner
(Germany)

SERVES 3–4

PREPARATION TIME 5 minutes

COOKING TIME 40 minutes

....

1 cup (250 mL) lager

1 cup (250 mL) water

1 cup (250 mL) white basmati rice, rinsed

½ Tbsp (7.5 mL) unsalted butter

¾ tsp (4 mL) kosher salt

SUBSTITUTING BEER FOR some (or all) of the water you use to cook rice adds a complexity that rice doesn't normally have. Light-bodied commercial beer is often made with rice for its clean, neutral flavour, so think of this recipe as being like adding a shot of flavour to light beer. I call for lager here, but if you're serving the rice with a spicy dish like the Spicy Lamb Rogan Josh (page 116) you could use a hoppier IPA for its bitter contrast to the curry's spice.

This recipe works just as well in a rice cooker.

Bring the beer and water to a boil in a medium saucepan. Stir in the rice, butter and salt. When the liquid returns to a simmer, cover the pot and cook for 20 to 25 minutes. When the rice is cooked, remove the pot from the heat and uncover. Let stand for 5 to 10 minutes.

NOTE Add frozen, shelled edamame (soybeans) with the rice for a more complete, lazy cook's dinner.

NOODLES

RECOMMENDED BEER
American-style India pale ale
Red Racer IPA, Central City Brewing
   (British Columbia)

SERVES 1

PREPARATION TIME 5 minutes

COOKING TIME 10 minutes

....

1 package dried noodles (single serving)

2 Tbsp (30 mL) peanut butter

½ tsp (2.5 mL) ground Szechuan pepper

1 Tbsp (15 mL) light soy sauce

1 Tbsp (15 mL) American-style India pale ale

1 Tbsp (15 mL) chili oil

1 scallion, finely sliced on the bias

¼ cup (60 mL) roasted peanuts, roughly chopped

THIS RECIPE IS written to serve one because I think it makes the perfect meal for nights when you don't feel like making something more elaborate. You can have it ready in less than 10 minutes and the noodles will probably be healthier than any ready-made freezer dinner. Obviously, it scales up nicely for a larger crowd.

The best noodles to use are Chinese instant noodles meant for dishes like chow mein. Look for ones that list only flour and water (or possibly also eggs) as ingredients. In a pinch it's fine to use the noodles from a package of instant ramen, but these are often sprayed with palm oil. Other types of Japanese instant noodles like udon are fine substitutes.

It is difficult to substitute for the unique, mouth-numbing flavour of Szechuan pepper. It stores relatively well if kept whole and ground as needed, so when you find some buy more than you need. If you can't find chili oil, substitute peanut or other vegetable oil with a pinch of red pepper flakes.

———— ⊰⊱ ————

Follow the package's instructions for preparing the noodles.

Place the peanut butter, Szechuan pepper, soy sauce, beer and chili oil in a bowl and microwave for 20 seconds. This will soften the peanut butter and make it easier to integrate with the rest of the sauce. Stir the sauce to blend, and add the cooked noodles. Stir vigorously to coat the noodles with the sauce. Garnish with the scallions and chopped peanuts.

SOBA SALAD

WITH SRIRACHA DRESSING

RECOMMENDED BEER
Schwarzbier or black lager
Dark 266, Cameron's Brewing
    (Ontario)

SERVES 4

PREPARATION TIME 20 minutes

COOKING TIME 10 minutes

· ·

SRIRACHA DRESSING

2 Tbsp (30 mL) sunflower oil

2 tsp (10 mL) toasted sesame oil

2 tsp (10 mL) Sriracha

4 cloves garlic, minced

¾-inch (2 cm) piece fresh ginger,
peeled and grated

¾ cup (185 mL) black lager

⅓ cup (80 mL) soy sauce

¼ cup (60 mL) maple syrup

3 Tbsp (45 mL) rice vinegar

1½ tsp (7.5 mL) cornstarch

juice of 2 limes

INGREDIENTS CONTINUE . . .

JAPANESE BUCKWHEAT NOODLES, or soba, make a particularly good base for a cold noodle salad. I was introduced to the concept for this salad by the *Rebar Modern Food Cookbook.* Be sure to not overcook the noodles and rinse them immediately under running cold water or they can easily become stodgy and lose all of their pleasant chew. Feel free to substitute other vegetables as they come into season. Corn, cherry tomatoes and sugar snap peas are all great options.

———— ❖ ————

SRIRACHA DRESSING For the dressing, heat the oils in a medium saucepan over medium heat until they start to shimmer, about 3 minutes. Add the Sriracha, garlic and grated ginger and sauté until fragrant, only about 1 minute. Pour in the beer, soy sauce, maple syrup and vinegar and whisk to combine. Bring the dressing to a simmer.

Meanwhile, prepare a slurry from the cornstarch and 2 tablespoons (30 mL) of cold water. When the sauce is simmering, pour in the cornstarch slurry and whisk to combine. Continue to gently simmer for 5 to 7 minutes so that the liquid reduces slightly and the cornstarch thickens the sauce. Take off the heat, whisk in the lime juice and refrigerate the dressing.

METHOD CONTINUES . . .

SOBA SALAD

1 lb (500 g) soba noodles

½ red onion, cut in thin, short slices

1 carrot, peeled and grated

¼ head napa cabbage, cored and thinly shredded

½ English cucumber, quartered, seeded and chopped

1 Tbsp (15 mL) sesame seeds

¼ cup (60 mL) cashews

¼ cup (60 mL) cilantro leaves

1 avocado, pitted, sliced and peel removed

SOBA SALAD Follow the instructions on the package for cooking the soba noodles. Set a large colander in your sink for draining the cooked noodles. Do not overcook the noodles. Taste a noodle 1 to 2 minutes shy of the prescribed time. As soon as they don't have any raw-noodle crunch in the middle, remove the pot from the heat and dump the noodles into the colander to drain. Run cold water over the noodles and once they're no longer scalding hot, toss the noodles so that all of them are exposed to the cold water. Drain thoroughly.

Combine the noodles and vegetables in a large serving bowl. Garnish the salad with sesame seeds, cashews and cilantro. Pour between half and two-thirds of the dressing over top and toss to coat.

Serve the salad with the sliced avocado on the side and the remaining dressing as a dipping sauce.

RISOTTO

WITH RED CABBAGE, BACON AND APPLES

RECOMMENDED BEER
Strong Belgian ale
Dernière Volonté, Microbrasserie
    Dieu du Ciel! (Quebec)
La Caracole Nostradamus,
    Brasserie La Caracole (Belgium)

SERVES 4–5

PREPARATION TIME 20 minutes

COOKING TIME 20 minutes

....

3⅔ cups (900 mL) chicken broth

2 bay leaves

3 sprigs thyme, chopped

3 pieces bacon, cut in chunks

1 yellow cooking onion, finely diced

1 large cooking apple, peeled, cored
and diced

10 oz (300 g) arborio rice

kosher salt

¾ cup (185 mL) Belgian ale

½ head red cabbage, cored and
shredded

2 cloves garlic, smashed and
minced

3 Tbsp (45 mL) unsalted butter

4 oz (125 g) grated Parmesan
(about 1 cup/250 mL)

freshly ground black pepper

T HE EXPANSION OF craft beer in Europe has moved in two
directions. While traditional beer cultures have thrived and
re-embraced beer styles and techniques that fell out of favour during
the industry's homogenization in the 20th century, other cultures
that were more usually connected to wine have started to embrace
beer. Italy has led the second category, with an industry of craft
brewers who often emulate the Belgian knack of making beer without
rules that goes well with food.

Risotto is a traditional Italian dish that features rice and a
creamy sauce based on fat, cheese and the rice's own starch. I have
adapted the standard technique so that the risotto can be made in
the oven and you need not stand by the stove stirring for eighteen
minutes. This risotto features red cabbage—one of those ingredients
that appear on many lists of foods that are difficult to pair with wine.

Heat your oven to 400°F (200°C); set a rack in the second-lowest
position.

In a medium saucepan, bring the chicken broth, bay leaves and
thyme to a simmer over medium heat.

Heat a Dutch oven over medium heat. Add the bacon pieces
and cook, stirring occasionally, until the bacon is somewhat crisp
and has rendered most of its fat. Remove the bacon and save it for
later. If there is more than about a tablespoon (15 mL) of fat, pour off
the excess.

Reduce the heat to medium-low and add the onion and
apple to the pan. Sweat, stirring to coat in bacon fat, until they are
soft and the onions are somewhat translucent, about 7 to 8 minutes.
Increase the heat to medium and add the rice with a pinch of kosher
salt. Toast for 3 to 4 minutes until the rice is fragrant. Pour in the

METHOD CONTINUES . . .

beer and scrape the bottom of the Dutch oven with a straight-edged wooden spoon to loosen any brown bits. Add the cabbage and garlic to the pan and stir to mix evenly. Pour the simmering broth through a sieve (to remove the herbs) into the Dutch oven. Cover tightly with the lid and move the Dutch oven to the oven to bake for 18 minutes.

After 18 minutes, open the oven and remove the lid. If most of the liquid has been absorbed, remove the pot from the oven. If not, replace lid and continue to cook for 2 to 3 more minutes. Stir in the butter, Parmesan, pepper to taste and reserved bacon, and let stand for a minute to melt the butter before serving.

NOTE If you want your cabbage to be particularly soft and entirely without a hint of crunch, blanch it in boiling water for 2 to 3 minutes at the start of the process.

BRAD CLIFFORD

Champion Homebrewer and Nanobrewer at Get Well Bar
Toronto, Ontario

THE HOBBYISTS WHO take up homebrewing are attracted to the activity for a diverse list of reasons. Some are looking for a way to apply a background in chemistry that is more fun than developing fertilizers, while others are taken in by the promise of beer for 50 cents a bottle. A large group, including Brad Clifford, who started brewing at home in 2009, started out aiming to recreate the flavour of their favourite styles of beer.

Clifford picked up a taste for hoppy ales at his local Toronto brewpubs, C'est What and (the now closed) Duggan's Brewery. Before IPAs really dominated retail shelves and were as common as they are now on beer lists, homebrewing was the quickest route to pale ale truly loaded with IBUs.

Based on the number of entries and variety of competitions, it's clear that homebrewers also enjoy the competitive nature of their hobby. Clifford quickly found a place on the figurative podium by winning the Best in Show award at the 2011 and 2012 Canadian Amateur Brewers Association Awards and also Homebrewer of the Year in 2012. He's quick to cite the example set by homebrewers like Mike Duggan, who successfully turned pro, as an inspiration for his early success.

Part of the prize for winning best in show at the CABA Awards is the opportunity to brew with the professionals at Beau's All Natural Brewing Company in Vankleek Hill, Ontario, for their CABA CABA Hey program. In his first time brewing with brewmaster Matthew O'Hara, they made just over 2,000 litres of Doublewide Double IPA. This American-style take on the double IPA came in at over 100 IBUs and 8 percent alcohol. Clifford's second session came after a major upgrade at Beau's, so they were able to make three times as much of the Mutineer Imperial Pilsner

that came out in February 2013. On top of scaling his recipes up
for the larger batch, he also had to adapt them to use only organic
ingredients, as is the standing rule at Beau's.

Clifford took his semi-pro experience to Toronto's Get Well
Bar, where he has helped open an in-house nanobrewery and set up
a two-hectolitre system. A batch size of two hectolitres is 200 litres
or, roughly speaking, 400 pints. That seems like quite a lot of beer
until you consider that the system at Beau's brews more than
7,000 litres in a batch.

The list of styles that Clifford has brewed at Get Well is a long
and varied one that ranges from Vienna lager to Belgian saison to an
English bitter. As a self-described hop head he keeps coming back
to pale ales like the Pinball Wizard American pale ale that was their
first brew. Whether brewing at home or the nanobrewery, it's the
ability to craft beers that meet his exacting standards that keeps him
interested.

SEAFOOD

Seafood and beer have a mutually beneficial relationship based largely on their variety and flexibility. For instance, mussels and salmon are both masters of carrying a wide variety of flavours that can be paired with a countless number of beers.

Light-flavoured white beers go well with the delicate, citrus-based sauces and seasonings that are often used with seafood. Hearty seafood dishes can be paired with darker beers that will complement their sweet flavours. Interestingly, dark and thick stout is a traditional, contrasting partner for briny, light-flavoured oysters.

POACHED SALMON

WITH MUSTARD PAN SAUCE

RECOMMENDED BEER
Belgian witbier
Dominus Vobiscum Blanche,
   Microbrasserie Charlevoix
   (Quebec)
St. Bernardus Blanche, Brouwerij St.
   Bernardus (Belgium)

SERVES 4

PREPARATION TIME 10 minutes

COOKING TIME 15-20 minutes

··

15 sprigs flat-leaf parsley, leaves
finely minced and stems reserved

1 orange, zested, cut into ¼-inch
(.5 cm) round slices (reserve zest)

½ red onion, thinly sliced and slices
quartered

1 cup (250 mL) witbier

4 salmon fillets

kosher salt

freshly ground black pepper

1 Tbsp (15 mL) whole-grain mustard

2 Tbsp (30 mL) unsalted butter,
cold and cut into small cubes

SALMON IS WIDELY available and has a mild but rich flavour. It's an accessible and delicious seafood main course that also has a good deal of underappreciated flexibility. High heat will crisp the skin, but steaming at a lower temperature will more clearly present its subtle flavours.

———— ⊁⊱⊰⊰ ————

Scatter the parsley stems, orange slices and onion slices over the bottom of a wide saucepan that has a tightly fitting lid. Pour the beer into the pan and turn the heat to medium. Bring to a gentle simmer.

Pat the salmon fillets dry with paper towels and season both sides with a pinch of salt and a few grinds of black pepper. Move the fish to the pan on top of the orange and onion slices. Cover and reduce the heat to low. Cook until the internal temperature of the largest fillet is 125°F (52°C). Start checking the temperature with a probe thermometer after about 10 minutes.

Move the fish to a platter and cover loosely with aluminum foil. Remove the orange slices and parsley stems and pour the liquid in the pan through a fine-mesh sieve into a measuring cup. Return the pan to medium heat and pour the strained liquid back into the pan. Add the mustard and cook for 2 minutes. Stir in the cubes of butter one at a time. Once the butter has melted, remove the pan from the heat and stir in the minced parsley leaves and orange zest, and season to taste with kosher salt and black pepper.

MUSSELS

RECOMMENDED BEER
Pilsner
Foothillz Pilz, Wildrose Brewery
   (Alberta)

SERVES 4

PREPARATION TIME 15 minutes

COOKING TIME 10–13 minutes

....

1 lb (500 g) mussels

3 cloves garlic, minced

2 tsp (10 mL) cumin seeds

¼ tsp (1 mL) freshly ground black pepper

¼ tsp (1 mL) cayenne

¼ cup (60 mL) pilsner

MUSSELS ARE THE underappreciated stars of the bivalve world. By preparing them at home you can feel more confident that they have been carefully picked over and dead ones (that could make you sick) discarded.

Mussels each carry a bit of seawater that releases into the pan when they open. When recipes add a bunch of liquid (usually wine, tomatoes or beer) to the pan, it just dilutes this delicious juice. The dry environment will also concentrate the flavours from the spice paste. By splashing the mussels with a bit of beer at the table the liquid will loosen any flavourful bits stuck to the pan and fill the room with a delicious, steamy aroma.

————— ❁ —————

Gently dump the mussels into a colander in your kitchen sink and rinse them with cold water. Look for any with broken shells, or open shells that don't close when the shell is tapped; discard these. Most cultivated mussels are carefully cleaned before they make it to the store, but if you find any that still have beards pull the beards off.

Use a mortar and pestle or the flat side of your chef's knife to make a paste from the garlic, cumin, black pepper and cayenne.

Heat a cast iron Dutch oven or large heavy pot with a tight-fitting lid over medium-high heat for 2 minutes. Transfer the mussels from the colander to the Dutch oven and replace the lid. After 4 minutes open the lid and spread the spice and garlic paste over the mussels. Replace the lid and shake gently to distribute the paste. Now is the time to have your guests seated at the table and ready to eat. Place a trivet or hot pad in the middle of the table.

After another 4 minutes of cooking, lift the lid and check to see if all of the mussels (more or less) have opened. If it looks like there are still several with closed shells, cook for another 2 to 3 minutes. Discard any whose shells haven't opened. Move the whole pot to the table and set it on the trivet. Once everyone has been warned that the sides are hot, carefully lift the lid and pour the beer over the mussels.

GRILLED

MOULES FRÎTES

RECOMMENDED BEER

Saison

Saison Station 55, Microbrasserie
 Hopfenstark (Quebec)

Saison Dupont Vieille Provision,
 Brasserie Dupont (Belgium)

SERVES 4–6

PREPARATION TIME 25 minutes

COOKING TIME 20 minutes

....

2 lb (1 kg) mussels

1 lb (500 g) mixed new potatoes,
washed

1 tsp (5 mL) fennel seeds

3 Tbsp (45 mL) olive oil

2 tsp (10 mL) kosher salt

freshly ground black pepper

A BOWL OF mussels served with Belgian frîtes (and mayonnaise) is one of the leading contenders for recognition as a national dish of Belgium. My adapted version of the traditional dish takes the classic combination—mussels and potatoes—and prepares them with that most familiar American cooking appliance, the backyard grill. With that approach we maintain the traditional ingredients—and flavours—of moules frîtes, but prepare them in an "at-home friendly" way.

Moules frîtes evolved in a culture that puts beer on an equal footing with wine as the default dinner-table beverage. Paired with this recipe, saison continues to make its case as one of the best food beers by complementing the herbal flavours and contrasting with the salinity.

We repeat the idea that dry heat (rather than steam) can be used to open mussels' shells and cook their flesh. A large part of the salty liquor that comes with a mussel will be lost through the grates, but the flavour account is at least partly balanced with the addition of the grill's smoke.

Serve with plenty of crusty sourdough bread.

Gently dump the bag of mussels into a colander in your kitchen sink and rinse them with cold water. Look for any with broken shells or with open shells that don't close when the shell is tapped and discard these. Most cultivated mussels are carefully cleaned before they make it to the store, but if you find any that still have beards, pull the beards off.

Hold the cleaned mussels in a large mixing bowl.

Set a large handful of hardwood chips (cherry or apple are ideal) to soak in water for 30 to 60 minutes. Drain water away and transfer chips to an 18-inch-long (45 cm) piece of aluminum foil. Gather the chips into a pile and fold the aluminum foil around the pile to form a closed packet. Use a fork to perforate the top side of the packet with 20 to 30 holes.

Bring a medium-large pot of salted water to a boil. Meanwhile, cut the potatoes in half. The most delicious part of the potato is the surface that will eventually be in contact with the hot oil, so keep the goal of maximizing the surface area of the cut face in mind as you decide which way to bisect each potato. Place the cut potatoes in the boiling water and cook for 10 to 12 minutes or until you can just barely slide a paring knife into them.

Once the potatoes are in the boiling water, you can head outside to deal with heating the grill. Lift the grate of your propane grill and place the wood chips packet on the metal bars or lava rocks that sit between the element and the cooking bars. Light the grill and heat it on high with the lid down for 8 minutes.

Back inside, transfer the parboiled potatoes from the hot water to a plate lined with paper towels. Dry thoroughly and transfer to a large mixing bowl. Add the crushed fennel seed, olive oil, kosher salt and several grinds of black pepper.

When the grill is heated and smoky, reduce the heat of all burners to medium. Open the lid and transfer the potatoes directly to the grill. Pour the mussels over top and use a pair of tongs to keep them in a pile. Close the grill's lid and cook for 4 to 5 minutes.

Have a large serving bowl and pair of long-handled tongs ready. Open the grill and start removing any mussels that have opened or potatoes that are well browned on the bottom. Periodically close the lid for 1 to 2 minutes to wait for the slower ones to cook. Once nearly all the shells are open, discard any mussels with unopened shells.

BRUSSELS
AND MUSSELS

RECOMMENDED BEER
Saison
Deliverance Saison, Great Lakes
    Brewing (Ontario)

SERVES 4

PREPARATION TIME 20 minutes

COOKING TIME 10–13 minutes

....

1 lb (500 g) mussels

1 lb (500 g) Brussels sprouts,
cleaned and trimmed

2 tsp (10 mL) olive oil

1 shallot or ½ small yellow cooking
onion, diced

½ tsp (2.5 mL) caraway seeds,
lightly toasted and lightly crushed

1 tsp (5 mL) orange zest

1 heaping tsp (5 mL) Dijon mustard

pinch red pepper flakes

1⅓ cups (330 mL) saison

kosher salt

freshly ground black pepper

crusty bread, toasted for serving

MUSSELS AND BRUSSELS sprouts share an important characteristic: they both are best cooked lightly with a certain attention to timing. Adding beer to the pot with the shellfish and vegetables creates a steamy environment that will cook the Brussels sprouts.

It's always important to clean mussels as thoroughly as possible, but in this case it's doubly so since any sand or grit will be picked up by the shredded sprouts and no one wants that.

Serve with a loaf of rustic, crusty bread torn into chunks and lightly toasted.

——————— ❯❯❯◀◀◀ ———————

Gently dump the bag of mussels into a colander in your kitchen sink and rinse them with cold water. Look for any with broken shells or with open shells that don't close when the shell is tapped and discard these. Most cultivated mussels are carefully cleaned before they make it to the store, but if you find any that still have beards, pull the beards off.

For the Brussels sprouts, I like to fill the kitchen sink or a large bowl with cold water. Working with one at a time, I trim the hard, woody stem end from each sprout and pick away any leaves that are old and grizzled or have black spots. The trimmed sprouts then go into the cold water. I find that my food processor, equipped with its slicing disc, is the most efficient way to shred the sprouts, but you could also use a sharp knife. If you go the knife route, you might want to leave the stem attached as a handle for holding the sprouts as you cut them. Either way, after they've been shredded they go back into the water, where I agitate them with my fingers to loosen any dirt that should sink to the bottom. Shift the shredded sprouts to a clean kitchen towel or salad spinner and carefully wring or spin to dry them.

METHOD CONTINUES . . .

Toss the clean mussels and shredded Brussels sprouts in a large bowl to combine evenly.

Heat the olive oil in a cast iron Dutch oven or large heavy pot with a tight-fitting lid over medium heat for 2 minutes. Add the diced shallot or onion and cook until softened and translucent, about 4 to 5 minutes. Add the caraway seeds, orange zest, red pepper flakes and mustard and stir to coat the onions. Immediately transfer the mussels-sprouts mixture into the pot and pour in the beer.

Clamp on the lid and continue to cook over medium heat until the mussels have opened. Start checking for cooked mussels at about the 7-minute mark after you put the lid on. Once nearly all the shells are open, discard any mussels whose shells remain closed. You may have to add 2 or 3 minutes to the cooking time, but mussels that stay closed after that were probably dead to start with and shouldn't be eaten.

Transfer the cooked mussels and sprouts to a bowl and serve. I like to serve the broth and sprouts that will be hanging out in the bottom of the pot with a chunk of toasted bread on the side.

FISH

RECOMMENDED BEER
English-style bitter
Red Racer ESB, Central City Brewing
   (British Columbia)

SERVES 4

PREPARATION TIME 20 minutes

COOKING TIME 8 minutes per batch

....

4 cups (1 L) rice bran oil

4½ oz (140 g) all-purpose flour
(about 1 cup/250 mL)

4½ oz (140 g) rice flour, extra for
dusting (about ⅔ cup/160 mL)

½ tsp (2.5 mL) baking powder

pinch salt

1⅔ cups (400 mL) English-style
bitter, cold

4 large Pacific cod or other
whitefish fillets, skin on

fine sea salt

lemon wedges for serving

THIS IS AN ideal case study where beer is equally critical as an ingredient and as the ideal partner for the finished dish. The carbonation helps lift and lighten the batter. Cold beer holds carbonation best, so this is one time when it is best to use it straight from the fridge.

Serve with chips, lemon wedges and Tartar Sauce (page 165) for a traditional fish 'n' chips meal.

———— ≫≫⋘ ————

Lay out two cookie sheets and place a wire rack on each. This rig will work both for letting excess batter drip away and to cool the fish once it comes out of the hot oil.

Set a Dutch oven over medium heat and fill with 2 inches (5 cm) of oil. Heat the oil to 375°F (190°C).

Pour the cold beer into a medium mixing bowl. Use a fine-mesh strainer to sift the flours into the beer. Add baking powder and salt and mix to combine, but be careful not to overmix. Dust the fish with rice flour. Dip each fillet into the batter and transfer to the hot oil. Don't overcrowd the pan; you may have to work in two batches.

Before flipping each fillet, use a ladle to add an extra dollop of batter to the top. This will give the crust added bits that will be light and crisp. Cook until dark golden brown and the fish reaches an internal temperature of 125°F (52°C), about 4 minutes per side. Hold the finished fillets on the clean wire rack and season, while still hot, with fine sea salt.

SEARED SCALLOPS

WITH PONZU SAUCE

RECOMMENDED BEER
American-style pale ale
Pale Ale, Steam Works Brewery
   (British Columbia)

SERVES 4 as an appetizer or
side dish

PREPARATION TIME 20 minutes,
plus 4–6 hours to marinate

COOKING TIME 15 minutes, plus
10 minutes to cool sauce

. . . .

6–8 medium to large scallops

⅓ cup (80 mL) American-style
pale ale

kosher salt

2 Tbsp (30 mL) grapeseed or other
neutral oil

PONZU SAUCE

⅓ cup (80 mL) beer from scallop
marinade

3 Tbsp (45 mL) soy sauce

1 Tbsp (15 mL) sugar

½ oz (15 g) bonito flakes (see Note)

1 Tbsp (15 mL) lime juice

TUNA WAS ALWAYS the textbook fish for everyone's Introduction to Half-Cooked Seafood class. When a chunk of bluefin loin is properly crusty on the outside and barely warm on the inside it shares the colour and texture of a rare filet mignon steak. Unfortunately, we've stripped almost all of these top-of-the-chain, big fish from the ocean and they are getting to be an unsustainable option, in the same category as Chilean sea bass.

Luckily, farmed Pacific scallops are a great alternative that have a firm, buttery texture and a subtle but sweet flavour.

———— ✻ ————

Gently rinse the scallops under cold running water and pat dry with paper towels. Place them in a resealable plastic bag with the beer and refrigerate for 4 to 6 hours.

Remove the scallops from the bag, reserving the beer for the sauce, and pat dry. Season each scallop with a pinch of kosher salt. Let stand while preparing the sauce.

Heat the oil in a heavy-bottomed, non-stick pan for 2 to 3 minutes. When the oil is just barely starting to smoke, sear the scallops on the first side until a golden brown crust develops, about 2 minutes. Flip to the other side and cook for 30 seconds more. Immediately remove to a plate and serve sliced thickly, with Ponzu Sauce for dipping.

To make the sauce, in a small saucepan set over medium heat, combine the beer, soy sauce and sugar. Cook, stirring occasionally, until just simmering and the sugar is dissolved completely. Pour into a small Mason jar (or other glass container with a tight-fitting lid) and add the bonito flakes. Move to the freezer to chill for 10 minutes.

Once the sauce is cool to the touch, add the lime juice, screw the lid on tightly and shake. Strain the sauce through a fine-mesh sieve into a serving bowl.

NOTE The goal is to flash-cook and sear the outside of the scallops while leaving the inside mostly raw. The best way to do this is to follow the times carefully.

Bonito flakes are shavings of dried, smoked bonito fish, usually found in Asian grocery stores.

MIRELLA AMATO

Master Cicerone and owner of Beerology
Toronto, Ontario

THE EVER-EXPANDING SELECTION of craft beer presents a problem and an opportunity. Sometimes there are just too many options available to make an easy choice and into that void step beer educators like Mirella Amato. Through her beer-related journalism for *Taps* magazine, CBC Radio and Beerology, her beer education and consulting company, she has been working for over six years to introduce craft beer to curious drinkers.

In October 2012, Amato became the first Master Cicerone in Canada and only the sixth in the world. A cicerone (pronounced sis-uh-rohn) is the beer world's analogue for wine's sommelier. The title is granted by the Cicerone Certification Program founded by Ray Daniels in 2007 through his Craft Beer Institute. According to the program's website, a Master Cicerone has an "encyclopedic knowledge of beer and a highly refined tasting ability." The idea is that they will be able to taste and identify beer, design beer lists, have a working knowledge of the brewing process, know about proper beer service and be experts on matching beer with food.

It's the highest of three certification levels, following Certified Beer Server and Certified Cicerone. At the time Amato received her designation, there were over 18,000 Certified Beer Servers worldwide but only 36 attempts (six successful) had been made for the third level. The test includes fourteen hours of written, oral and tasting exams spread over two days.

Amato is also one of only ten Canadian national level judges recognized by the Beer Judge Certification Program. BJCP judges are recognized for their expert tasting ability and act as the official judges for sanctioned homebrewing and professional brewing competitions.

Beerology is Amato's company, through which she operates guided beer tastings and beer dinners, and provides consulting and training services to breweries and restaurants. The one piece of advice that she finds herself repeating to audiences of beer newcomers is that beer needs to be poured into a glass to fully appreciate its complexities. It was by people drinking it straight from the bottle that beer got its reputation as a filling, gassy beverage.

Amato has been closely involved with professional networks for women in beer, stretching back to her attendance at the first meeting of the Pink Boots Society—a group that describes itself as "the female movers and shakers in the beer industry"—in 2008.

From her professional designations and North America–wide recognition, it's clear that Amato is one of Canada's top craft beer experts. As the appreciation for full-flavoured beer expands to new corners of the market, she's still happy to work with small audiences and see the look on people's faces as they try craft beer for the first time.

MEAT AND POULTRY

From Braised Smoky Ribs to spicy Grilled Jerk Chicken, this section is a collection of meat recipes that have strong flavours to match strong beers. By this point on the menu, you'll probably be ready for stouts, a hoppy IPA or even a sour ale.

Often, meat dishes are paired with a strong sauce, and together those need a strong beer to complement. Brown ales are one exception where a relatively subtle beer is paired with meat, because the roasted malt flavours match well with roasted meat flavours. If you're choosing a beer for a meat recipe and the first flavours that come to mind when describing the dish don't have to do with spice (or smoke), it's probably best to find a beer that depends on malt for its flavour.

Sausages

IN SPICED BEER SAUCE

RECOMMENDED BEER
Dunkel weiss
Dunkel, Denison's Brewing
   (Ontario)
Altbairisch Dunkel, Brauerei
   Ayinger (Germany)

SERVES 4–6

PREPARATION TIME 10 minutes

COOKING TIME 45 minutes

. . . .

4 bratwurst sausages

1 Tbsp (15 mL) canola oil (or other neutral cooking oil like grapeseed or sunflower)

½ yellow cooking onion, finely minced

6 gingersnaps or other spiced cookie, crushed but not totally atomized

1 Tbsp (15 mL) capers, drained and chopped

1 cup (250 mL) dark beer

1 tsp (5 mL) lemon juice

pinch kosher salt

black pepper

I**N NORTH AMERICA** we associate sausages with our propane or charcoal grill. Even if I'm going to eventually grill a sausage, I start by poaching it in water for two reasons. First, this means that I can use either fresh or frozen sausages (just add 10 minutes to the cooking time if defrosting is needed). And secondly, it's much easier to control how quickly heat enters meat when working with hot water instead of hot air or metal. The objective is a caramelized, snappy skin and juicy meat. Too often just-grilled sausages are charred and desiccated.

When I'm in the mood for an aromatic prelude to my meal, I'll throw a crushed (skin on) garlic clove and a bay leaf into the water. Because the sausage casing is only semi-permeable, the expanding filling pushes outward more forcefully than the water pushes in and the time window is short, there is almost no chance that any of the flavours in the water will make it into the meat. A kitchen that smells like garlic and bay leaf is an aromatic appetizer, though.

If you make your own sausages (kudos), the goal for your bratwurst recipe—unlike many Italian sausages—is to have a fine, smooth texture and a subtle, refined flavour that depends almost totally on the delicious marriage of salt and pork.

———— »»»««« ————

Arrange the sausages in the bottom of a wide sauté pan. Cover with cold water by about an inch (2.5 cm). Put the lid on the pan and turn the heat to high. When wisps of steam start to escape from under the lid and the water is barely simmering, reduce the heat to low. Poach the sausage in the barely simmering water for 20 minutes.

Remove the sausages from the pan, pour the water out and wipe the inside of the pan. Return it to medium heat and add the oil. Once the oil is hot, return the sausages to the pan and brown them on all

METHOD CONTINUES . . .

sides—about 2 to 3 minutes per side. Keep the sausages warm on a heated platter, tented loosely with aluminum foil.

Cook the minced onion and cookie crumbs in the pan until softened, about 5 minutes. Add the chopped capers, stir to combine and cook for a minute. Pour the beer into the pan and increase the heat to medium-high. Scrape any accumulated deliciousness from the bottom and sides of the pan. Bring to a simmer and cook for 5 minutes. Take off the heat, stir in the lemon juice, a pinch of salt and a few grinds of black pepper.

Pour the sauce over the sausages and serve with pickles, mustard and sauerkraut.

NOTE A staggering mountain of sausage recipes direct the home cook to poke holes in the sausage casing. The idea is that this relieves pressure and keeps the skin from bursting. I'm very skeptical. It seems to me that this just helps fat and delicious juices to escape. Good-quality sausages that aren't packed with fillers and that use natural casings will almost never split. It especially helps if you follow this process of poaching the sausages before browning the outside.

CURRYWURST

RECOMMENDED BEER
Märzen-Oktoberfest
Night-Märzen, Beau's All-Natural
   Brewing (Ontario)
Oktober Fest-Märzen, Brauerei
   Ayinger (Germany)

SERVES 4

PREPARATION TIME 10 minutes

COOKING TIME 35–40 minutes

....

2 Tbsp (30 mL) vegetable oil

1 small yellow onion, minced

1 tsp (5 mL) mustard seeds

1 Tbsp (15 mL) curry powder

¾ cup (185 mL) ketchup

1 Tbsp (15 mL) tomato paste

1 tsp (5 mL) Worcestershire sauce

¼ cup (60 mL) cider vinegar

4 fresh Mexican chorizo sausages

¼ tsp (1 mL) black pepper,
freshly ground

¼ tsp (1 mL) nutmeg

CURRYWURST IS THE near-official street food of Berlin. The sauce is a strange (but delicious) brew of American and British ingredients: ketchup, Worcestershire sauce and curry powder. These came to Germany with the Allied soldiers stationed in postwar Berlin.

Bockwurst or bratwurst are the most likely types of sausage for a street vendor in Berlin to sell with currywurst sauce. These veal-and-pork sausages can be difficult to find in North America, and in truth I prefer to serve a more heavily spiced sausage, like Mexican-style chorizo fresco or a spicy Italian sausage, with currywurst sauce. The sausages are sliced on the bias into diagonal chunks (some street vendors in Berlin have gone so far as automating this part of the process). This dish is best enjoyed with friends and plenty of beer. As a dish with so many vibrant, loud flavours, currywurst is a natural match for a craft beer with a touch of malty sweetness and refreshing hops.

———— ✦✦✦ ————

Light your propane grill and heat it on high with the lid down for 15 minutes.

While the grill is heating, start the currywurst sauce. Heat a medium saucepan over medium-high heat for 2 minutes. Pour in the oil and then add the diced onion and mustard seeds. Cook the onions, stirring occasionally, until they have softened, about 4 to 5 minutes. Add the curry powder to the onions and stir to coat; cook for 1 to 2 minutes or until very fragrant. Pour in the ketchup, tomato paste, Worcestershire sauce and cider vinegar. Bring to a simmer and reduce heat to low until the sauce thickens, about 15 minutes.

While the sauce simmers, clean the grill bars with a metal brush and reduce the heat of one unit to low and the other(s) to medium. Place the sausages over the cooler element. Cook, turning

METHOD CONTINUES . . .

occasionally, until the internal temperature reaches 160°F (71°C). Depending on your grill, this can take between 15 and 25 minutes.

When the sauce has thickened, turn heat off and cover. Add black pepper and nutmeg just before serving with sliced sausage.

NOTE Currywurst sauce can be made several days ahead of time. If making ahead or storing leftovers, keep the sauce refrigerated in a tightly sealed container.

CHOUCROUTE GARNI

RECOMMENDED BEER
Belgian pale ale
Cuvée Houblonnée IPA Belge,
　Microbrasserie À la Fût (Quebec)

SERVES 6–8

PREPARATION TIME 20 minutes

COOKING TIME 1 hour 15 minutes

....

2 Tbsp (30 mL) olive oil

7 oz (200 g) pork belly or unsmoked side pork, skin off, thickly sliced and cut into 2-inch (5 cm) strips

4 links garlic sausage

3 medium yellow cooking onions, peeled and thinly sliced

4 whole garlic cloves, skin off, lightly crushed and root end removed

kosher salt

1 cup (250 mL) Belgian-style pale ale

4 lb (1.8 kg) sauerkraut

1 smoked ham hock (optional)

10 dried juniper berries

2 bay leaves

2 cups (500 mL) homemade stock or low-sodium chicken broth

4 links smoked sausage

black pepper

CHOUCROUTE IS ONE of the principal dishes from the large catalogue of Alsatian recipes. In Alsace it is typically prepared and served with Riesling or another dry, fruity white wine, but the dish is also popular in Antwerp, where beer stands in for the wine.

This is a case where the recipe is more of a concept than a specific set of instructions. The idea is to find really good sauerkraut (or make your own); cook it with spices, beer and some carefully selected pork products; and then serve it as a delicious, steaming pile of goodness with boiled potatoes and several types of mustard. So, for instance, if you can't find traditional cold-smoked montbeliard sausage, an equivalent amount (by weight) of kielbasa will do, or if you can't get fresh pork belly, then good-quality bacon will be fine.

Serve with boiled potatoes, a variety of mustards, and a loaf of crusty bread.

———————— ❧ ————————

Heat the olive oil in a large enamelled Dutch oven or casserole set over medium heat. After 2 minutes, add the chopped pork belly and garlic sausage. Cook, stirring and turning occasionally, until the meat is light-golden brown. Remove the pork belly and sausages to a plate. Pour the fat out of the pot into a small bowl. Reserve 2 tablespoons (30 mL) for the next step and discard the rest.

Pour the reserved fat back into the Dutch oven (still over medium heat) and dump in the onions, garlic cloves and a large pinch of kosher salt. Stir occasionally and cook until the onions have softened and given up some of their moisture. Pour in the beer and scrape the bottom of the pan to deglaze. Add the sauerkraut, ham hock, juniper berries, bay leaves and chicken broth. Once the liquid is gently bubbling, season with black pepper, cover the pot and reduce the heat to low. Cook for 30 minutes.

METHOD CONTINUES . . .

Return the pork belly and garlic sausage to the pot along with the smoked sausage. Replace the lid and cook for another 35 to 45 minutes.

Remove the bay leaves. Use tongs to move the sauerkraut to the centre of a large heated platter, leaving most of the cooking broth behind in the pot. Cut the sausages into manageable pieces and arrange these chunks around the outside of the platter. Place the ham hock on top of the sauerkraut. The broth can be served with crusty bread for dipping.

NOTE If your sauerkraut tastes particularly sour or salty to you, fill a large bowl with cold water and rinse the kraut in it.

CARBONADE FLAMANDE

[STOOFVLEES]

RECOMMENDED BEER
Belgian oud bruin, or sour brown
Oud Bruin, Yaletown Brewing
(British Columbia)
Supplication, Russian River Brewing
(United States)

SERVES 4–6

PREPARATION TIME 30 minutes
(more if you buy a whole piece of
beef and cut it up yourself)

COOKING TIME 3 hours

....

2 Tbsp (30 mL) unsalted butter

1 lb (500 g) beef shoulder, chuck,
blade or stewing beef, cut into
1-inch (2.5 cm) chunks

2 medium onions, peeled, cut in half
through the poles and thinly sliced

bouquet garni (bay leaf, 4–5 sprigs
thyme, 5 dried juniper berries)
(optional)

1⅓ cups (330 mL) Belgian sour
brown or abbey dubbel beer, 2 Tbsp
(30 mL) reserved

3–4 slices whole wheat bread

whole-grain mustard

2 tsp (10 mL) brown sugar

1 Tbsp (15 mL) cider vinegar (omit if
you use a sour beer)

kosher salt

pepper

THIS SIMPLE, HEARTY stew from Belgium is carried by two main flavours: beef and beer. The onions, herbs and mustard sing along in the background, but the other two get the solos.

Like most traditional stews, this one started as a peasant dish made with chunks of inexpensive beef and the drink usually at hand. In this case it was sour Belgian brown ale. The meat is easy enough to find—ask for chuck or shoulder, or find a package marked as chuck, shoulder, blade or stewing beef. Sour ales are one of the last styles to really catch on, even in the craft beer market. Lambic is the fairly well-known umbrella under which the sour, spontaneously fermented beers of Brussels are categorized. They are almost always blended and sold as the lightly coloured gueuze. The darker, more rustic oud bruin is really what's called for here, but acceptable substitutes are a "sour brown" or a dark Belgian dubbel. The dubbel has the colour and dark fruit flavours we want, but since it lacks the acid edge we'd need to add a bit of vinegar to the stew.

The mustard gives the recognizable heat and flavour. Use whatever type you like best (brown, Dijon or grainy), just not yellow ballpark, please. Since the bread will thicken the stew and add more roasted grain flavours, it should be dark and rustic; both pumpernickel and dark rye will do just as well as whole wheat.

The name of this recipe is a bit of a sticking point. For whatever reason, it's the French name that has crossed into English, but since the dish is native to the Flemish parts of Belgium it makes more sense to refer to it by its Flemish name, stoofvlees. Calling it carbonade is like calling tourtière "Quebec meat pie" or gumbo "sopa de quingombo."

Traditionally, this dish is served with frîtes or boiled potatoes, but you might also want to add a simple green vegetable.

METHOD CONTINUES . . .

Over medium heat, melt the butter in a cast iron or enamelled Dutch oven or a heavy stockpot. Season the beef chunks with kosher salt. When the butter stops foaming, transfer the meat to the pan and brown on at least two sides, for 3 to 4 minutes per side. It's critical to work in batches and err on the side of more, smaller batches, since meat in a crowded pan will only steam and stew rather than developing a delicious brown crust.

After the last round of beef is out of the pan, knock the heat down a notch or two to medium-low and add the onions. Cook until soft and translucent and just beginning to colour, stirring occasionally with a straight-edged wooden spoon, about 7 to 9 minutes. While the onions are cooking, prepare your bouquet garni by tying the bay leaf, thyme and juniper berries (if using) into a cheesecloth package.

Pour the beer into the pan (holding aside 2 Tbsp/30 mL) and scrape the delicious brown bits off the bottom of the pan with a wooden spoon. Once the liquid is simmering, return the beef to the pan with the bouquet garni. Cover with a tight-fitting lid, reduce heat to low and cook for about 2 hours.

As the 2-hour mark approaches, spread the bread with mustard. Remove the lid from the Dutch oven and place the bread on top of the stew with the mustard side down. Replace the lid and continue for another 30 minutes or until the bread falls apart and thickens the stew. Stir once or twice.

Five minutes before serving, remove the bouquet garni and stir in the brown sugar, vinegar (if using), reserved 2 tablespoons (30 mL) of beer and a few grinds of black pepper. Taste for seasoning and add salt if you like.

Pie

RECOMMENDED BEER

English brown ale

10W30 Brown Ale, Neustadt
   Springs Brewery (Ontario)

SERVES 4-6

PREPARATION TIME 30 minutes

COOKING TIME 4 hours

. . . .

FILLING

14-16 Pickled Onions (page 173) or
good-quality store-bought pickled
onions

3 Tbsp (45 mL) unsalted butter

2 lb (1 kg) beef (shin, oxtail or
chuck), cubed and dusted with flour

4 slices thick-cut bacon, cut into
1-inch (2.5 cm) pieces

2 cups (500 mL) English brown ale

2 cups (500 mL) beef broth
(or chicken broth)

3-4 sprigs fresh thyme

1 bay leaf

12-14 cremini mushrooms, wiped
with a damp paper towel and halved

½ cup (125 mL) frozen green peas

1 large carrot, peeled, cut in
small dice

freshly ground black pepper

kosher salt to taste

INGREDIENTS CONTINUE . . .

THIS PUB CLASSIC is a good candidate for a lazy Sunday afternoon at home. The aroma of slowly stewing beef is usually one of the most delicious smells that can fill a kitchen. Add bacon and pickled onions to the chorus and mouths will water for hours.

The consensus pick from my research and testing for best cut of beef to use in this dish is beef shin. Even if you're working with a full-service butcher, shin can be a difficult cut to locate.

I picked up the idea for using pickled onions from Valentine Warner's recipe in his book *The Good Table,* which came to me via an excellent blog post on the *Guardian* website that compared various recipes for steak and ale pie. If you really don't like the idea of pickled vegetables right in with everything else, go ahead and submit yourself to the dreary chore of peeling 20 or so baby onions.

Usually a pie like this would be topped with a thick flour-and-fat crust. But it also would usually be made with beef left over from the Sunday roast or made by the dozens for pub customers. Obviously, if we're going to our butcher to find shin, we're engaging in a different sort of operation here. Since the biscuits don't need to be dropped on until well into the cooking, we still have access to the pot and that means the beef can cook for hours and the carrots can go in near the end so they keep a pleasant texture.

———— ⁂ ————

FILLING Soak the pickled onions in ice water for between 10 and 30 minutes, depending on how wary you are of a slight vinegar edge to certain bites.

Heat your oven to 300°F (150°C); set a rack in the second-lowest position.

Over medium heat, melt 2 tablespoons (30 mL) of the butter in an enamelled Dutch oven. Divide the beef into at least two batches

METHOD CONTINUES . . .

BISCUIT TOPPING

½ cup (125 mL) milk

1 tsp (5 mL) lemon juice

8 Tbsp (120 mL) unsalted butter, melted

8½ oz (260 g) flour (about 2 cups/500 mL)

2 tsp (10 mL) baking powder

½ tsp (2.5 mL) baking soda

1 tsp (5 mL) kosher salt

2¼ oz (68 g) shredded cheddar cheese (about ½ cup/125 mL)

½ cup (125 mL) English brown ale, cold

and put the first batch into the pan once the butter stops foaming. Cook the beef until deep brown and caramelized, approximately 6 to 8 minutes, turning once or twice. Remove to a bowl and repeat with the second batch.

Drain the onions and add to the fat in the Dutch oven along with the bacon. Cook, stirring occasionally, until the onions have started to brown and the bacon has rendered some of its fat, about 7 minutes. Remove the onions and bacon from the pan and pour the beer in to deglaze the pan. Scrape the brown bits off the bottom of the pan with a straight-edged wooden spoon. Add the browned beef, and the browned onions and cooked bacon, back to the Dutch oven. Add the broth, sprigs of thyme and bay leaf. Cover the Dutch oven and move it to the heated oven.

Cook with the lid on for 2 hours. Remove the lid from the Dutch oven and cook, uncovered, for another hour.

Meanwhile, melt the remaining tablespoon (15 mL) of butter in a medium saucepan over medium-high heat. When the butter has just started to darken, add the mushrooms and toss to coat. Sauté until they have shrunk noticeably and turned dark golden brown. Set aside.

BISCUIT TOPPPING To prepare the biscuit topping, in a medium bowl, whisk the milk and lemon juice together and let stand at room temperature for 15 minutes so that the milk clabbers. Melt the butter and let cool slightly. In a large bowl, whisk together the flour, baking powder, baking soda, salt and cheese. Add the melted butter and the beer to the clabbered milk, and stir. Pour the wet ingredients into the dry and use a wide spatula to fold them together until just combined.

At the end of the hour of uncovered cooking, remove the thyme and bay leaf from the Dutch oven. Increase the oven temperature to 400°F (200°C). Add a few grinds of black pepper and taste the sauce for seasoning. If necessary, add a large pinch of kosher salt. Stir the frozen peas, diced carrots and sautéed mushrooms in with the meat.

Use a ¼-cup (60 mL) disher or ice cream scoop to drop dollops of the biscuit batter on top. Leave some space between the biscuits for steam to escape. Return the pot to the oven and cook for 45 more minutes.

Let the pie stand at room temperature for 15 minutes before serving.

NOTE If you don't make your own pickled onions, good-quality cocktail onions will do fine, but pickled cippolini are even better.

RIBS

RECOMMENDED BEER

Smoked beer

Rauchbier, Central City Brewing
  (British Columbia

Aecht Schlenkerla Rauchbier Märzen,
  Brauerei Heller-Trum (Germany)

SERVES 4

PREPARATION TIME 30 minutes,
plus 2–8 hours after applying the rub

COOKING TIME 4 hours

....

2 racks spareribs

3⅓ oz (100 g) brown sugar, lightly
packed (about ½ cup/125 mL)

⅔ oz (20 g) kosher salt
(about 2 Tbsp/30 mL)

1½ Tbsp (22.5 mL) chili powder
(⅓ oz/12 g)

3 star anise, just the seed pods, ground

¼ tsp (1 mL) cayenne

½ cup (125 mL) orange juice

¼ cup (60 mL) smoked beer

½ tsp (2.5 mL) pure vanilla extract

RIB SAUCE

3 Tbsp (45 mL) ketchup

1 Tbsp (15 mL) maple syrup

¼ cup (60 mL) smoked beer

¼ tsp (1 mL) cayenne

2 Tbsp (30 mL) cider vinegar

kosher salt

MEMBERS OF THE traditionalist school of southern barbecue demand ribs that are both smoky and chewy. They want to leave teeth marks after taking a bite. To them, falling off the bone is strictly for pork shoulder. I think the world of pig cookery is big enough to handle two styles of ribs and these are moist and delicious. The smoky element comes with the rauchbier in the braising liquid.

Serve with coleslaw and Warm Potato Salad with Summer Sausage (page 46).

Remove the ribs from their packaging and lay them on a cutting board with the meat side down and the bones facing up. If the skirt of meat is still attached, use a sharp knife to remove it. Discard or save it for another use. Use the point and dull side of a thin-bladed knife to lift the membrane away from the bones. Carefully work your finger under the membrane, remove the knife, and pull the membrane off and discard.

Mix the brown sugar, kosher salt, chili powder, star anise and cayenne together in a small mixing bowl. Lay a piece of aluminum foil that is at least 6 inches (15 cm) longer than the rack of ribs out on your counter. Place racks on the foil and scatter about a quarter of the dry spice rub on the bone side of the ribs, flip them over and press the remaining rub into the meat side. Bring the long sides of the foil together and crimp them over 2 or 3 times, but not tightly against the ribs. Do the same with one of the short sides, crimping it tightly against the end of the racks of ribs. Form the open end of the package into an ad hoc funnel. Move the package to the bottom half of a broiler pan and refrigerate for between 2 and 8 hours.

Heat your oven to 350°F (175°C); set a rack in the middle position. Remove the broiler pan from the refrigerator. In a 2-cup

(500 mL) measure, whisk together the orange juice, beer and vanilla extract. Pour into the open end of the foil package. Place the broiler pan in the preheated oven and cook for one hour. Reduce the heat to 250°F (120°C) and continue to cook for 2 more hours.

Set a large, wide saucepan over your stove's largest burner. Remove the ribs from the oven and use a pair of kitchen tongs to carefully hold the foil package over the pan. Snip the bottom corner of the package with kitchen shears so that the braising liquid can drain into the pan. This is the base for the rib sauce. Leave the ribs wrapped in the foil while you make the sauce.

Turn the heat under the pan to medium-high and add the ketchup, maple syrup, beer and cayenne to the braising liquid. Whisk frequently until the liquid comes to a simmer. Simmer vigorously to reduce the sauce until it is thick enough to coat the back of a wooden spoon, about 10 minutes.

While the sauce is simmering, turn your broiler to high and move an oven rack to the second-highest position. Place the ridged top half of the broiler pan onto the bottom; spray with cooking spray. When the sauce is close to reduced, remove the ribs from the foil; place them meat side up on the broiler pan.

Stir the vinegar into the sauce. Taste and add salt if necessary. Use a kitchen brush to paint the top of the ribs thickly with sauce and place them under the broiler. After 3 minutes, repeat the brushing process and give the ribs another 1 or 2 minutes under the broiler. The sauce on the ribs will become sticky and caramelized, but watch closely to ensure it doesn't burn.

Use kitchen shears to cut the ribs into 2- or 3-bone pieces.

NOTE If you don't have heavy-duty aluminum foil, you should use two layers of the standard gauge.

STOUT-BRAISED

Lamb Shank

RECOMMENDED BEER

Stout

Déesse Nocturne, Microbrasserie
   Dieu du Ciel! (Quebec)

SERVES 4-6

PREPARATION TIME 30 minutes

COOKING TIME 4 hours

....

3 lb (1.5 kg) lamb shanks
(roughly 1 shank per person)

flour for dusting meat

2 Tbsp (30 mL) olive oil

2 yellow cooking onions, diced

1 carrot, peeled and diced

1 stalk celery, diced

5 garlic cloves, minced

1½ cups (375 mL) stout

1½ cups (375 mL) chicken broth

2 bay leaves

4 sprigs rosemary

2 large parsnips, peeled, cut in large
dice

1½ cups (375 mL) green peas

1½ Tbsp (22.5 mL) tomato paste

kosher salt

freshly ground black pepper

THE LINES BETWEEN stew, meat pie and braised whole cut aren't always obvious. In this case, the lamb shank makes for an interesting, somewhat primitive presentation. The stout paired with the lamb is a great example of deep, rich, roasted flavours complementing each other.

Heat your oven to 325°F (160°C); set a rack in the second-lowest position.

Dry the shanks with paper towel and season with kosher salt and freshly ground black pepper. Dust the meat lightly with flour.

Heat the olive oil in a flame-proof, oven-safe Dutch oven or casserole, over medium heat for 2 minutes. Brown the shanks on all sides in the hot oil, 2 to 3 minutes a side. Depending on the size of your casserole, you may have to do this in two batches. Remove the browned lamb to a large plate. Add the diced onions, carrot and celery to the pot and stir to coat. Cook for 5 to 7 minutes or until the vegetables barely start to colour. Add the minced garlic to the pan with the other vegetables and cook until fragrant, about 30 seconds.

Increase the heat to medium-high and immediately pour in the stout. Use a straight-edged wooden spoon to scrape any browned bits from the bottom of the pan. Add the chicken broth, bay leaves and rosemary and bring the liquid to a simmer before returning the meat to the pan. It's more important that the meaty ends of the shanks are all nestled down in the liquid and okay if the bony ends are uncovered. Put the lid on the casserole and move it to the heated oven.

Cook, covered, for 3 hours. Remove the pot from the oven and increase the oven temperature to 375°F (190°C). Remove the shanks from the pan and hold them on a clean platter. Discard the bay leaves and sprigs of rosemary. Add the diced parsnips, peas and tomato paste to the Dutch oven and stir so that the tomato paste dissolves. Return the meat to the pot and put the pot back in the oven, uncovered this time. Cook for 35 to 45 minutes or until the shanks are well browned and the sauce has reduced. Taste the sauce and add kosher salt or black pepper as needed.

Serve with polenta and sautéed rapini or spinach.

NOTE If you want to make this dish the day before, reheat in a 325°F (160°C) oven, covered, for 20 to 30 minutes.

SPICY LAMB

ROGAN JOSH

RECOMMENDED BEER
India pale ale
Mad Tom IPA, Muskoka Brewery
(Ontario)
Latitude 48 IPA, Samuel Adams
(Boston Beer) (United States)

SERVES 6

PREPARATION TIME 25 minutes,
plus 4–6 hours to marinate

COOKING TIME 3 hours

....

LAMB MARINADE

6 cloves garlic, peeled and minced

thumb-sized piece of fresh ginger,
peeled and grated

¼ cup (60 mL) yogurt

½ tsp (2.5 mL) black pepper,
freshly ground

2 lb (1 kg) boneless lamb shoulder,
cut in large cubes

A CRAFT-BREWED IPA is a much better match for Lamb Rogan Josh than the pale international lagers that are brewed in India. Spicy Indian curries are one of the best opportunities for beer to spread its wings. All of the citrus and pine resin spice of an IPA matches very well with the spices in the dish.

Serve with warm naan bread and plenty of Basmati Rice Steamed with Beer (page 70).

LAMB MARINADE In a medium mixing bowl, combine the garlic, ginger, yogurt and black pepper and stir to combine. Add the cubed lamb and toss to coat in the yogurt mixture. Cover the bowl with plastic wrap and refrigerate for 4 to 6 hours.

ROGAN JOSH Heat your oven to 300°F (150°C); set a rack in the second-lowest position.

Blitz the turmeric, red onions, red peppers and dried chilies in a food processor until a chunky paste forms.

Place an enamelled Dutch oven over medium heat. Toast the coriander seeds, cardamom pods, fennel seeds, cumin seeds and cloves for 2 to 3 minutes or until fragrant. Grind the toasted spices in a spice grinder or mortar and pestle.

Pour the oil into the already hot Dutch oven. Reduce the heat to low, add the onion paste mixture and the ground spices and cook, stirring frequently, until the mixture has darkened slightly, about 10 to 12 minutes. Add the tomatoes, lamb and its marinade, salt, cinnamon stick and bay leaves. Add enough water to the reserved tomato liquid to bring it to a cup full (250 mL) and pour this into the pot. Stir the pot's contents and cover before moving it into the heated oven.

ROGAN JOSH

1 tsp (5 mL) turmeric

3 medium red onions, peeled and halved

2 red peppers, halved, seeded and roughly chopped

3 dried chilies (chile de arbol or cayenne), seeds shaken out

4 tsp (20 mL) coriander seeds

1 Tbsp (15 mL) green cardamom pods

1 tsp (5 mL) fennel seeds

1 tsp (5 mL) cumin seeds

5 cloves

1 Tbsp (15 mL) sunflower oil (or other neutral vegetable oil)

one 14-oz (398 mL) can diced tomatoes, liquid drained and reserved

2 tsp (10 mL) kosher salt

1 cinnamon stick

2 bay leaves

1 tsp (5 mL) garam masala

2 fresh red chilies, seeded and thinly sliced

¼ cup (60 mL) cilantro leaves, minced for garnish

Cook for 2 ½ to 3 hours or until the lamb is very tender and the sauce has reduced slightly. Remove the cinnamon stick and bay leaves from the pot and discard. Off the heat, stir in the garam masala and garnish with chilies and cilantro.

NOTE If you have an abundance of fresh tomatoes, substitute 5 plum tomatoes for the canned.

JERK CHICKEN

RECOMMENDED BEER
American-style pale ale
Crazy Canuck Pale Ale, Great Lakes
   Brewery (Ontario)
Pale Ale, Sierra Nevada Brewing
   (United States)

SERVES 6

PREPARATION TIME 15 minutes,
plus at least 8 hours to marinate

COOKING TIME 26–28 minutes

. . . .

6 chicken leg quarters

MARINADE

1 Tbsp (15 mL) allspice berries

1 Tbsp (15 mL) black peppercorns

½ cinnamon stick

5 or 6 sprigs of fresh thyme,
leaves stripped

1¼-inch (3 cm) piece of fresh
ginger, grated

1 garlic clove, chopped

3 green onions, chopped roughly

2 Scotch bonnet chilies, stemmed,
most of the seeds knocked out, and
chopped

1 Tbsp (15 mL) dark brown sugar

1½ tsp (7.5 mL) kosher salt

2 Tbsp (30 mL) soy sauce

juice of one lime

THIS DISH IS much too spicy for most wines—both in the chili heat sense and in the ginger and allspice way. The recipe doesn't call for beer as an ingredient, but beer will be, far and away, the best partner. The citrus zest flavours from the pale ale will complete the bright, vibrant profile of this meal.

Spicy food and hot weather go well together because the capsaicin in chilies is an irritant that causes us to perspire. As the sweat evaporates our body temperature moderates. Along with the fact that hot peppers grow well in hot weather, this is why hot-weather countries tend to have spicier food.

Jerk chicken is the well-known Jamaican dish that makes excellent use of the backyard grill. I'd rather calibrate a jerk rub so that spices and meat share the spotlight, with the peppers as backup singers. You can serve extra hot sauce on the side for the hardcore chili heads. Pressing the jerk rub under the skin of the chicken leg quarters is worth the extra effort. I recommend wearing latex gloves when working with hot peppers. Even if you're careful about keeping your hands away from your eyes, if a seed comes in contact with a cut or scrape, or even under a fingernail, it can really ruin your evening.

———— ❯❯❯❮❮❮ ————

For the marinade, in a small dry pan toast the allspice, peppercorns and cinnamon over medium heat. You want to activate the volatile oils in the spices and will know they're ready when the kitchen fills with their aroma. This will take anywhere from 3 to 6 minutes. Remove the spices to a mini food processor. Add the thyme, grated ginger, garlic, green onions and chilies, and blitz until a smooth paste forms. Add the sugar, salt, soy sauce and lime juice and pulse a couple of times to combine.

Pat the chicken legs dry with a paper towel and arrange in one layer in the bottom of a wide, low dish. Pour the marinade over the chicken. For each piece of chicken, lift the skin near where the thigh and leg meet and work some of the spice mixture under the skin. Cover with plastic wrap and refrigerate for 8 hours or overnight.

In your kettle grill, light a chimney full of lump charcoal. When it is white hot, bank it to one side and add another handful of charcoal. Put the lid on the kettle and let the heat even out over 5 minutes or so.

Brush the marinade off the outside of the chicken pieces, but leave any that is under the skin where it is. Sear the chicken, skin side down, over the hot side of the grill for 2 minutes. Flip and move it to the cool side of the grill, as far away from the heat as possible. Replace the lid and cook for 18 minutes. Flip the chicken back over so that the skin is against the grill again and cook until the internal temperature reaches 165°F (74°C), about 6 to 8 minutes. Remove from the grill and serve.

Propane variation: Preheat your grill on high for 15 minutes. Turn one side as low as it will go, and then sear the chicken over the hot side and cook it the rest of the way over the low side.

Indoor variation: Heat your oven to 350°F (175°C). Spray an oven-safe glass lasagna pan or casserole with non-stick spray and arrange chicken pieces in a single layer in the bottom of the pan. Cover with aluminum foil and cook until the internal temperature reaches 160°F (71°C), about an hour. Finish by searing in a very hot cast iron skillet for 2 minutes a side. Do the searing in two batches.

METHOD CONTINUES . . .

NOTE Skin-on, bone-in leg quarters (pieces where the drumstick is attached to the thigh) stand up best to the heat of grilling. A large package of drumsticks will feed a party quite well, though. If you just can't handle dark meat, buy skin-on, bone-in breasts and cut them in half so that they take a bit less time to cook and won't dry out as much. Also, even if you have a dedicated spice grinder or second coffee grinder for spices, it can pick up "off" flavours and the nooks are difficult to clean with soap and water. The best way to clean a spice grinder is by pulsing a small handful of uncooked white rice 5 or 6 times.

FRIED CHICKEN

RECOMMENDED BEER
Sour ale (Sour beers are still relatively rare in Canada, but many craft breweries are starting to experiment with them. You may have to go to the brewery and buy this one directly in bottles or growlers.)
Dulcis Succubus, Le Trou du Diable (Quebec)
Gueuze Lambic, Brasserie Cantillon Brouwerij (Belgium)

SERVES 4 to 6

PREPARATION TIME 50 minutes (in 2 stages), plus overnight in brine

COOKING TIME 20 minutes

....

BRINE

2 cups (500 mL) water

1 lemon, cut in eighths

10 sprigs thyme

10 black peppercorns

1¾ oz (50 g) kosher salt

1 whole chicken (3-4 lb/1.5-1.8 kg)

1 lb (500 g) ice

INGREDIENTS CONTINUE . . .

FRIED CHICKEN IS one of the culinary world's greatest pop hits. The dual contrasts of texture—between crunchy crust and succulent chicken—and flavour—salty and spicy outside against the rich, fatty inside—are nearly perfect. All that's missing is an element of sour that most recipes try to supply by adding buttermilk to the crust. A glass of sour wild ale goes better with the meal than a cold, frosty buttermilk, but maybe that's just me?

There may have been a time when home cooks used the same wide, cast iron frying pan to cook eggs, bacon and fried chicken. This is one time when I'm all in favour of departing from tradition. For safety's sake you need to use a pot that is at least 4 inches (10 cm) tall. Cast iron Dutch ovens are great (enamelled or not) and a heavy, stout stockpot will work as well.

Serve with coleslaw and Smoky Collard Greens (page 62).

———— ❀ ————

BRINE Set a large saucepan over high heat and pour the water into it. Add the lemon, thyme, peppercorns and kosher salt to the water. Bring the water to a gentle boil and reduce the heat to medium-low. Cook for 5 to 10 minutes, stirring occasionally to dissolve the salt and encourage the aromatic flavours to move into the water. Move the pot off the heat and let cool, uncovered, for 15 to 20 minutes.

Meanwhile, cut the chicken into 10 pieces: that's 2 drumsticks, 2 thighs, 4 breast quarters and 2 wings. Remove the wing tips and discard or save them with the back bone for making chicken stock. Place a large resealable bag in a large measuring cup or bowl and fill with the pound (500 g) of ice. Pour the warm brine and all of its contents over the ice. Add the chicken to the bag, seal and refrigerate for 6 to 8 hours or overnight.

METHOD CONTINUES . . .

FOR FRYING AND DREDGING

4 cups (1 L) rice bran oil (or peanut oil or other neutral oil)

12½ oz (390 g) flour (about 3 cups/750 mL)

2 Tbsp (30 mL) fine sea salt

2 Tbsp (30 mL) garlic powder

1 Tbsp (15 mL) paprika

1 tsp (5 mL) freshly ground black pepper

½ tsp (2.5 mL) cayenne

½ tsp (2.5 mL) Hop Salt (optional, recipe on page 161)

1⅓ cups (330 mL) sour ale, cold

⅔ cup (160 mL) table cream, cold

fine sea salt for seasoning

Lay out two cookie sheets and place a wire rack on each. This holding rig will work both for letting excess batter drip away and to cool the chicken once it comes out of the hot oil.

FRYING AND DREDGING Set a cast iron Dutch oven or other heavy-bottomed pot with sides that are at least 4 inches (10 cm) tall over medium heat. Pour in enough oil to come about 1 inch (2.5 cm) up the side. Use an instant-read, deep-fry or non-contact thermometer to maintain the oil's temperature between 340°F and 350°F (171°C and 175°C). Set your oven to 225°F (105°C), or 250°F (120°C) if that's its lowest setting.

Whisk together the flour, sea salt, garlic powder, paprika, black pepper, cayenne and hop salt (optional) in a medium mixing bowl. Move one-third of the seasoned flour mixture into a large pie plate or other wide dish and the other two-thirds into a second pie plate. In a medium mixing bowl, combine the sour ale and cream. Remove the chicken from the brine, rinse very briefly under cold running water and thoroughly pat dry with paper towels.

Lightly dredge the chicken pieces in the first pie plate, shake off excess flour and move them to the holding rig. Dunk each piece in the beer-cream mixture and then drop them into the second pie plate where they should be rolled to thoroughly coat in seasoned flour.

Increase the heat under the oil-filled pot slightly and add the dredged thighs to the hot oil. Use your thermometer and stove setting to keep the temperature of the oil between 350°F (175°C) and 370°F (188°C). After 2 minutes, add the dredged drumsticks to the oil. Fry, turning each piece once, until the crust is dark golden brown, about 8 more minutes. Place the thighs (skin side up) and drumsticks on the second holding rig, season them very lightly

METHOD CONTINUES . . .

with fine sea salt and move the cookie sheet into the preheated oven.
Move the breast quarters and wings to the hot oil and fry as with
the other pieces for about 6 minutes. Season them very lightly and
transfer them to the oven (also skin side up) where they can be held
until you're ready to eat, up to 15 minutes. The chicken should reach
an internal temperature of 165°F (74°C).

NOTE If you don't want to break down a whole chicken, this recipe
will work just as well with all legs, thighs or halved breasts.

SWEETS AND DESSERTS

There is absolutely no reason to cast beer aside because we have reached the end of the meal. It works excellently as an ingredient in baked recipes and other desserts. Very generally speaking, the only rule is that the beer should be sweeter than the dessert.

Dark-flavoured beers will go well with baked desserts. I'm a particular fan of sour beers, and fruit lambics, especially ones that are off-dry, match nicely with fruit-based desserts. This type of beer is still relatively difficult to find, so it's fortunate that these desserts will also pair well with slightly rich, mildly bitter styles like abbey dubbels.

Gingerbread

RECOMMENDED BEER
Porter
Coffee Porter, Mill Street Brewery
(Ontario)

SERVES 6

MAKES 8-inch (20 cm) square pan;
cuts into 16 squares

PREPARATION TIME 25 minutes

COOKING TIME 35–40 minutes,
plus at least 1 hour to cool

....

¾ cup (185 mL) porter

½ tsp (2.5 mL) baking soda

⅔ cup (160 mL) fancy molasses

4 oz (120 g) dark brown sugar,
firmly packed (about ½ cup/125 mL)

½ cup (125 mL) granulated sugar

6½ oz (195 g) flour
(about 1½ cups/375 mL)

2 tsp (10 mL) ground ginger

1 scant tsp (5 mL) kosher salt

½ tsp (2.5 mL) ground cinnamon

½ tsp (2.5 mL) baking powder

2 eggs

⅓ cup (80 mL) vegetable oil

CAKE-STYLE GINGERBREAD is a world away from the hard, dry cookies and desiccated houses that make an appearance at Christmas. Put simply, it's actually a pleasure to eat. A dark porter adds a complex layer to the flavour and the carbonation helps add lightness. Obviously, the nearly black colour also darkens the cake.

Serve warm or at room temperature on its own or with a dollop of whipped cream, made using the beer for this recipe and the technique in the Blueberries with Dark Abbey Ale Whipped Cream (page 133).

——————— ⧓ ———————

Heat your oven to 350°F (175°C); set a rack in the middle position. Prepare an 8-inch (20 cm) square cake pan by buttering and flouring its sides.

Set a medium saucepan over medium heat and pour in the porter. Bring to a boil and remove from the heat. Stir in the baking soda. After the science-project volcano foaming settles down, stir in the molasses and both the sugars.

In a large mixing bowl, whisk together the flour, ground ginger, kosher salt, cinnamon and baking powder.

Transfer the porter-molasses mixture to a 4-cup (1 L) measure or medium mixing bowl. Whisk in the eggs and oil until thoroughly combined. Pour a third of the wet ingredients into the dry and whisk vigorously. Repeat with the other two-thirds, in two separate additions. This is not a recipe where you need to worry about creating gluten by overmixing. Whisk vigorously.

Pour the batter into the prepared pan, using a wide spatula to encourage stragglers. Bake the gingerbread for 35 to 40 minutes or until a cake tester, inserted in the centre, comes out mostly clean. Cool the cake in the pan on a wire rack for at least an hour, then slice into 2-inch (5 cm) squares.

NOTE All dry spices stay fresh longer if purchased as whole seeds or pods. That isn't an option with dried ginger—particularly problematic because of how wan stale dried ginger tastes—so it's important to replenish your supply regularly. I find it's best to buy from bulk stores in small quantities.

Cheese Course

HERE ARE SOME OF MY
FAVOURITE PAIRINGS

Fresh goat cheese with fruit beer

Mild, firm goat or sheep cheese with wheat beer

French Camembert with bière de garde or saison

Aged cheddar with hoppy bitter American-style pale ale

Creamy blue cheese with double IPA

Smoked Gouda or cheddar with imperial stout

Smoked blue cheese with smoked beer

Aged blue cheese with aged barley wine

CHEESE IS ONE of my favourite ways to end a meal. It's not sweet or baked, but deserves special attention. Craft beer's ability to pair with cheese is one of its secret weapons in the fight against wine dominance.

This is a good place for a reminder to pay attention to serving temperature. Most types of cheese are at their best at cool room temperature and beer is at its best between 41°F and 54°F (5°C and 12°C).

I'm sure it's obvious to even the most casual reader that I love cheese, but actually I think the problem with most cheese plates is too much choice, not too little. After dinner at home or a casual meal with friends, I think it's better to serve one well-chosen option, such as aged Stilton, paired with a single beer, perhaps an aged English barley wine, than to worry about satisfying various fickle tastes. Even for a party dedicated to beer and cheese, I think that three or four options in both categories are a good maximum.

BROWNIES

WITH SPICED ALE CHOCOLATE SAUCE

RECOMMENDED BEER
Spiced ale
Lions Winter Ale, Granville Island
    Brewing (Molson Coors) (British
    Columbia)

MAKES 9- × 13-inch (3.5 L) pan;
cuts into 24–32 brownies

PREPARATION TIME 35 minutes

COOKING TIME 25 minutes, plus
4–6 hours to cool

....

¼ cup (60 mL) unsalted butter,
plus more for greasing baking dish

6 oz (175 g) semi-sweet baking
chocolate, chopped

4½ oz (140 g) flour
(about 1 cup/250 mL)

½ cup (125 mL) good-quality cocoa

5 eggs

14 oz (400 g) brown sugar, lightly
packed (about 2 cups/500 mL)

1 tsp (5 mL) vanilla extract

½ tsp (2.5 mL) kosher salt

SPICED ALE CHOCOLATE SAUCE

1 cup (250 mL) spiced winter ale

2 Tbsp (30 mL) butter, cut into
small cubes

2 oz (60 g) semi-sweet baking
chocolate, chopped

A DARK IMPERIAL STOUT in this thick sauce would crank up the dark chocolate and roasted coffee flavours even further—and if that's your thing, go ahead and adapt—but I like the relative lightness of the spiced ale. When it comes to brownies, I prefer complexity to full throttle.

———— ❧ ————

Heat your oven to 350°F (175°C); set a rack in the middle position. Prepare a 9- × 13-inch (3.5 L) glass baking dish by greasing the inside surfaces with cold butter.

In a small saucepan, melt the butter over low heat. When the butter is hot and has stopped frothing, remove from the heat and immediately add the chocolate. Stir with a wooden spoon so that the heat from the butter melts the chocolate. We're trying to melt the chocolate without the added hassle of a double boiler, so careful attention and gentle heat are critical. If the chocolate won't melt off the heat, briefly return the pan to the burner, stir and watch it until it does melt. Pour into a bowl and set aside to cool.

Sift the flour and cocoa together into a medium mixing bowl. In a larger mixing bowl, combine the eggs, sugar, vanilla extract and salt. Use a stand mixer (with whisk attachment), hand mixer or whisk to beat ingredients until they are combined and the batter falls from the whisk in thick ribbons. Use a wide spatula to fold in the cooled butter-chocolate mixture. Quickly and gently fold in the flour mixture. In both folding steps be careful not to overmix or jostle the air from the batter, but also be sure to get right down to the bottom of the bowl.

Pour the batter into the greased pan and smooth the top with a spatula. Bake for 25 minutes until the top surface is cracked and set but still yielding to the touch. Start making the sauce while the

METHOD CONTINUES . . .

brownies are baking. Cool the brownies completely, in the pan, on a wire rack.

To make the sauce, set a medium to large saucepan over medium heat and pour the beer into it. Cook until the beer has been reduced by half. Be prepared for it to foam up as it heats, and reduce heat if necessary.

Once the beer is reduced, turn the heat down to low and whisk in one cube of butter at a time until melted. Do the same with the chocolate, working in small batches. Once the chocolate is melted, remove the pan from the heat and let stand for 1 minute. Pour sauce over brownies. The sauce should be thin enough that you can evenly distribute it over the brownies by lifting the pan and tilting it from side to side and front to back. Cool to room temperature before cutting into squares.

BLUEBERRIES

WITH DARK ABBEY ALE WHIPPED CREAM

RECOMMENDED BEER
Abbey dubbel
Dominus Vobiscum Double,
    Microbrasserie Charlevoix
    (Quebec)
Westmalle Trappist Dubbel,
    Brouwerij der Trappisten van
    Westmalle (Belgium)

SERVES 4

PREPARATION TIME 10 minutes

....

1 cup (250 mL) whipping cream,
cold

1 Tbsp (15 mL) sugar

2 Tbsp (30 mL) oak-aged ale

1 pint (500 mL) blueberries

....

Pictured on page 129.

THE GREATEST CHALLENGE from a pint of in-season blueberries (especially the wild ones) is to resist eating them by the handful. They deserve a simple, uncomplicated presentation that doesn't get in the way of their perfect tart-sweet balance. The best solution— that works as well for other slightly acidic fruit like strawberries and raspberries—is to serve them with a generous dollop of doctored whipped cream.

Beer picks up soft notes of vanilla from oak barrels and a touch of vanilla is dessert's answer to a pinch of salt or squeeze of lemon juice.

———— ⟫⟪ ————

Cream is easier to whip if everything is cold, but unless you're whisking by hand it's sufficient to make sure that the cream has been refrigerated for at least 8 hours.

Pour the cold cream into a medium mixing bowl. Immerse a hand blender's beaters in the liquid and turn it to medium-high. Beat at this speed until ridges start to form and the cream looks like it has some substance. Turn the blender off and test to see if the cream will hold soft peaks (points will form where the beaters leave the surface, but they will quickly bend over). Add the sugar and beer and mix just enough to combine. Taste and add more sugar if desired.

Divide the blueberries among four bowls and top each with a dollop of whipped cream.

NOTE The beer you use for the recipe will also be a great accompaniment for the dessert.

RICE PUDDING (RIJSTPAP)

WITH BRAISED PEACHES

RECOMMENDED BEER
Abbey dubbel
Terrible, Microbrasserie Unibroue
 (Sapporo) (Quebec)
Chimay Premiere (Red), Bières de
 Chimay (Belgium)

SERVES 5-6

PREPARATION TIME 10 minutes
(longer if you use fresh peaches)

COOKING TIME 35 minutes

....

5 oz (150 g) medium-grain rice
(about ¾ cup/185 mL)

4 cups (1 L) whole milk

pinch kosher salt

½ cinnamon stick

1 tsp (5 mL) pure vanilla extract

¼ cup (60 mL) sugar

BRAISED PEACHES

one 14-oz (398 mL) can of peaches
in natural juices

1⅓ cups (330 mL) dark abbey ale

½ cinnamon stick

¼ tsp (1 mL) freshly grated nutmeg

scant ¼ cup (60 mL) brown sugar,
lightly packed

FRÎTES, CHOCOLATE, MUSSELS and waffles are recognizable foods of Belgium. Rice pudding (rijstpap) deserves a spot on that list as well. This dessert works well on crisp September evenings at the end of peach season, or even better in February with good-quality canned peaches.

———— ❧ ————

In a strainer, rinse the rice under cold running water. Place in a sturdy, heavy-bottomed pan over medium-high heat with the milk, salt and cinnamon stick. Bring to a gentle boil and then reduce heat to low and cover. Simmer for 30 minutes, stirring occasionally.

While the rice is cooking, separate the peaches from their juice and simmer them in a separate saucepan with the beer, cinnamon stick, nutmeg and brown sugar. The fruit will need to cook for about 30 minutes uncovered, or until the liquid has reduced enough to thickly coat the peaches.

When the rice has been simmering for about half an hour, remove the lid and stir in the vanilla and sugar. Simmer for 5 more minutes. Remove the cinnamon and serve with stewed peaches on top.

NOTE In-season ripe fresh peaches can also be used. The peaches braised in beer would also make an excellent accompaniment for roast pork.

ice cream

RECOMMENDED BEER
Oak-aged ale
Barrel-Aged Imperial Porter, Central
   City Brewing (British Columbia)

MAKES 4 cups (1 L)

PREPARATION TIME 5 minutes

COOKING TIME 25 minutes, plus
8 hours to chill

1⅓ cups (330 mL) oak-aged ale

8 egg yolks

1 cup (250 mL) sugar

2 cups (500 mL) cream

1 cup (250 mL) milk

¼ tsp (1 mL) kosher salt

¼ tsp (1 mL) freshly grated nutmeg

WITH ITS MALTY sweet base and notes of toffee and vanilla that come from wood-cask aging, old ale is a natural for an ice cream base.

If you have room in your freezer, put a large mixing bowl in to chill.

Pour half of the beer into a wide saucepan set over medium heat. Bring to a simmer and cook for 5 to 8 minutes, or until reduced by half. Pour the reduced beer back in with the unreduced. You should have about 1 cup (250 mL) total.

Beat the egg yolks and sugar together using a hand mixer (or a stand mixer fitted with the whisk attachment) until they are lighter in colour and fall from the beater in ribbons.

Heat the cream and milk in a large, high-sided saucepan set over medium heat until the mixture barely reaches a simmer at 180°F (82°C). Pour the cream mixture in small doses into the egg mixture and whisk vigorously to combine. The idea is to slowly raise the temperature of the eggs (while lowering the temperature of the hot liquid) so that they don't scramble.

Return the mixture to the large saucepan and reduce the heat to low. Cook the custard until it reaches 180°F (82°C). Have the large (chilled, if possible) mixing bowl standing by with a fine-mesh sieve resting on its lip. Use a straight-edged wooden spoon to stir the custard, being careful to get right to the bottom of the pan and around the edges. As soon as it reaches 180°F (82°C), immediately remove the custard from the heat and pour it through the sieve into the bowl. Whisk in the beer, kosher salt and nutmeg.

Refrigerate the ice cream base for at least 8 hours before following your ice cream maker's instructions on churning it.

BANANA HEFEWEIZEN

CUSTARD

RECOMMENDED BEER
Hefeweizen
Hefeweizen, Tree Brewing (British Columbia)

SERVES 4–6

PREPARATION TIME 10 minutes

COOKING TIME 25 minutes

....

2 cups (500 mL) milk (whole is best, but 2% is fine)

1 cup (250 mL) hefeweizen

¼ cup (60 mL) sugar

2 Tbsp (30 mL) cornstarch

4 very ripe bananas plus 2 barely ripe bananas, thinly sliced into coins (reserve one coin per serving if making the garnish)

3 whole eggs plus 1 egg yolk

2 Tbsp (30 mL) freshly squeezed lemon juice (about half a lemon's worth)

½ tsp (2.5 mL) vanilla extract

½ tsp (2.5 mL) freshly grated nutmeg

GARNISH

6 mint leaves

1 Tbsp (15 mL) unsalted butter

¼ cup (60 mL) brown sugar

COOKED CUSTARDS are made in the home kitchen much less often than they were 30 or 40 years ago. Part of the reason, I bet, is that custard doesn't announce the host's skill and effort to dinner party guests the way a multilayer cake or complicated trifle do.

Custard recipes that call for beer are not very common. I had two inspirations for this recipe: hefeweizen displays notes of banana flavour that will be a welcome (if subtle) supporting player here, and I'm happy to offer any excuse to drink beer with dessert.

———— ❧ ————

Heat the milk, beer, sugar and cornstarch in a medium saucepan over medium-low heat until the liquid barely simmers.

Meanwhile, in a medium mixing bowl mash the 4 very ripe bananas with a sturdy potato masher. Add the 3 whole eggs, the egg yolk and the lemon juice and stir to combine. Pour about a quarter of the milk mixture another into the banana-egg mixture and quickly stir with a wooden spoon. Once the first addition is integrated, add another quarter, stir again, and so forth. The idea is to slowly raise the temperature of the egg mixture (while lowering the temperature of the milk mixture) so that the eggs don't scramble.

Pour the custard back into the saucepan, stir in the sliced banana coins and bring back to a simmer. Add the vanilla extract and grated nutmeg and stir again.

To make the garnish, set a small saucepan over medium heat. Add the butter to the pan. Once the bubbling stops, add the brown sugar. Stir to combine and cook until the sugar dissolves. Carefully add the reserved banana coins and sauté until brown and caramelized, about 3 minutes per side. Divide the custard into 4 glasses. Garnish each with a banana coin and a mint leaf, and serve.

NOTE For the very ripe bananas, it's fine to use frozen bananas that have been defrosted in the refrigerator overnight.

IPA ICE CREAM

WITH PRALINES

RECOMMENDED BEER
American-style India pale ale
Hops and Robbers, Double Trouble
    Brewing (Ontario)

MAKES 4 cups (1 L)

PREPARATION TIME 5 minutes

COOKING TIME 25 minutes, plus
8 hours to chill

1⅓ cups (330 mL) India pale ale

8 egg yolks

1 cup (250 mL) sugar

2 cups (500 mL) cream

1 cup (250 mL) milk

2 Tbsp (30 mL) maple syrup

¼ tsp (1 mL) kosher salt

PRALINES

½ cup (125 mL) pecan halves

3 Tbsp (45 mL) light brown sugar

1 tsp (5 mL) vegetable oil

pinch of salt

THE IMMEDIATELY RECOGNIZABLE hop bitterness of the IPA (think grapefruit zest and pine needles) is balanced by maple syrup in the base as well as the sweet pralines. That said, this ice cream is definitely one for the hop heads. The process for making pralines can be complicated (involving sugar being cooked with cream or evaporated milk to a "soft ball stage"). This is a simple process—but I think if you're going to the trouble of making your own ice cream, it's okay to cheat a bit on the garnish.

———— »»»««« ————

If you have room in your freezer, put a large mixing bowl in to chill.

Pour half of the beer into a wide saucepan set over medium heat. Bring to a simmer and cook for 5 to 8 minutes, or until reduced by half. Pour the reduced beer back in with the unreduced. You should have about 1 cup (250 mL) total.

Beat the egg yolks and sugar together using a hand mixer (or a stand mixer fitted with the whisk attachment) until they are lighter in colour and fall from the beater in ribbons.

Heat the cream and milk in a large, high-sided saucepan set over medium heat until the mixture barely reaches a simmer at 180°F (82°C). Pour the cream mixture in small doses into the egg mixture and whisk vigorously to combine. The idea is to slowly raise the temperature of the eggs (while lowering the temperature of the hot liquid) so that they don't scramble.

Return the mixture to the large saucepan and reduce the heat to low. Cook the custard until it reaches 180°F (82°C). Have the large (chilled, if possible) mixing bowl standing by with a fine-mesh sieve resting on its lip. Use a straight-edged wooden spoon to stir the custard, being careful to get right to the bottom of the pan and around the edges. As soon as it reaches 180°F (82°C), immediately remove the custard from the heat and pour it through the sieve into the bowl. Whisk in the beer, maple syrup and kosher salt.

Refrigerate the ice cream base for at least 8 hours before following your ice cream maker's instructions on churning it.

To make the pralines, place the pecan halves in a wide non-stick pan and barely cover with cool water. Turn the heat to medium-high and bring the water to a simmer. Pour the water away and return the pan to the heat. Add the brown sugar, oil and salt and toss to coat. Cook until the sugar caramelizes and the nuts are fragrant. Transfer the nuts to a cutting board (be very careful: the sugar is very hot and sticky) to cool before chopping them.

Follow your ice cream maker's instructions for adding the pralines. You may need to churn them in near the end or fold them in once the ice cream is frozen.

ice cream

RECOMMENDED BEER
Imperial oatmeal stout
St-Ambroise Oatmeal Stout,
   Brasserie McAuslan (Quebec)

MAKES 4 cups (1 L)

PREPARATION TIME 5 minutes

COOKING TIME 25 minutes, plus
8 hours to chill

....

1⅓ cups (330 mL) oatmeal stout

8 egg yolks

1 cup (250 mL) sugar

2 cups (500 mL) cream

1 cup (250 mL) milk

1 Tbsp (15 mL) honey

¼ tsp (1 mL) kosher salt

4 oz (125 g) good-quality semi-
sweet chocolate, chopped into
chip-sized pieces

THIS VERSION OF beer ice cream is aimed squarely at those who like their dessert to be dark and rich. The base gets its chocolate flavour from the dark roasted malts in the stout.

If you have room in your freezer, put a large mixing bowl in to chill.

Pour half of the stout into a wide saucepan set over medium heat. Bring to a simmer and cook for 5 to 8 minutes, or until reduced by half. Pour the reduced beer back in with the unreduced. You should have about 1 cup (250 mL) total.

Beat the egg yolks and sugar together using a hand mixer (or a stand mixer fitted with the whisk attachment) until they are lighter in colour and fall from the beater in ribbons.

Heat the cream and milk in a large, high-sided saucepan set over medium heat until the mixture barely reaches a simmer at 180°F (82°C). Pour the cream mixture in small doses into the egg mixture and whisk vigorously to combine. The idea is to slowly raise the temperature of the eggs (while lowering the temperature of the hot liquid) so that they don't scramble.

Return the mixture to the large saucepan and reduce the heat to low. Cook the custard until it reaches 180°F (82°C). Have the large (chilled, if possible) mixing bowl standing by with a fine-mesh sieve resting on its lip. Use a straight-edged wooden spoon to stir the custard, being careful to get right to the bottom of the pan and around the edges. As soon as it reaches 180°F (82°C), immediately remove the custard from the heat and pour it through the sieve into the bowl. Whisk in the beer, honey and kosher salt.

Refrigerate the ice cream base for at least 8 hours before following your ice cream maker's instructions on churning it, as well as for adding the chocolate chunks. You may need to churn them in near the end or fold them in once the ice cream is frozen.

GRANOLA

WITH SPENT GRAIN

MAKES about 6 cups (1.5 L)

PREPARATION TIME 10 minutes

COOKING TIME 30 minutes

....

3 cups (750 mL) spent grain (any kind), drained

7¾ oz (222.5 g) dark brown sugar, lightly packed (about 1 cup/250 mL)

½ cup (125 mL) maple syrup

¼ cup (60 mL) olive oil

½ tsp (2.5 mL) kosher salt

2 cups (500 mL) rolled oats

1 cup (250 mL) whole roasted, unsalted almonds

1 cup (250 mL) chopped walnuts

1 cup (250 mL) pumpkin seeds

¾ cup (185 mL) sunflower seeds

¼ cup (60 mL) flax seeds

½ cup (125 mL) raisins

½ cup (125 mL) dried cranberries

¼ cup (60 mL) dried cherries (optional)

THIS RECIPE COMBINES a delicious balance of sweet flavours and crunchy textures. Also, it puts the spent grain left after homebrewing to good use.

As is, the recipe is calibrated with a sweetness level that is best suited for breakfast. If you'd rather use it as a dessert garnish—perhaps a crunchy ice cream topping—you may want to increase the brown sugar and maple syrup by half and omit the seeds.

———— ❱❱❱❰❰❰ ————

Heat your oven to 350°F (175°C); set racks in the two middle positions. Line two cookie sheets with parchment paper.

Spread the spent grain over one of the cookie sheets and bake in the oven until dry, about 5 minutes.

Set a small saucepan over medium heat and combine the brown sugar and maple syrup. Stir until the sugar dissolves. Remove the pan from the heat and stir in the olive oil and kosher salt.

In a very large mixing bowl, combine the spent grain, rolled oats, almonds, walnuts, pumpkin seeds, sunflower seeds and flax seeds. Pour the sugar mixture over top and toss to coat thoroughly. Divide between the two lined cookie sheets and bake in the oven for 20 minutes, stirring twice. The granola should be dark and fragrant, but be careful not to burn the edges. Return to the mixing bowl and let cool slightly before adding the raisins, dried cranberries and dried cherries.

Stored in an airtight container, the granola will last for weeks, if not months.

NOTE Feel free to substitute or omit different nuts or seeds, depending on preference and allergies.

Oatmeal Raisin Cookies

WITH SPENT BARLEY

MAKES 2 dozen cookies

PREPARATION TIME 15 minutes

COOKING TIME 23–26 minutes, plus 1 hour to cool

....

½ lb (250 g) unsalted butter, softened

7¾ oz (222.5 g) light brown sugar, lightly packed (about 1 cup/250 mL)

¾ cup (185 mL) granulated sugar

2 eggs

6½ oz (195 g) flour (1½ cups/375 mL)

1 scant tsp (5 mL) kosher salt

½ tsp (2.5 mL) baking powder

1½ cups (375 mL) spent barley, drained

1½ cups (375 mL) rolled oats

1 cup (250 mL) raisins

HOMEBREWERS WHO HAVE moved up to the all-grain version of their hobby will have noticed that after sparging (the final rinse of the malted grains to remove their sugars) they are left with a pile of spent barley. Aside from feeding a backyard pig (or compost pile), spent barley can be put to practical use by baking with it. It is important that most of the liquid is drained from the barley.

This recipe makes delicious cookies that are just as excellent if wheat (or, not surprisingly, oats) was included in the grain bill for your original beer recipe.

———————— ❯❯❯❰❰❰ ————————

Heat your oven to 350°F (175°C); set racks in the two middle positions. Line two cookie sheets with parchment paper.

Using a hand mixer or the paddle attachment of a stand mixer, cream the butter, brown sugar and white sugar together until the colour and texture are lighter. This may take up to 3 minutes. Beat in one egg at a time.

In another bowl whisk together the flour, salt and baking powder. Use a wooden spoon to stir the flour into the butter mixture. Pour the spent barley, oats and raisins into the bowl and stir them in. Use a disher or two tablespoons to form the dough into 2-inch (5 cm) balls and arrange them on the lined cookie sheets.

Bake for 23 to 26 minutes or until the edges of each cookie look brown and crispy. Rotate and exchange the position of the sheets halfway through cooking. Use the parchment paper to slide the cookies onto a cooling rack and let them cool for at least an hour.

NOTE If you're not a homebrewer, you should give it a shot, but until then you can substitute another cup and a half (375 mL) of rolled oats for the spent barley.

SPINNAKERS GASTRO BREWPUB AND GUESTHOUSES

Paul Hadfield, Publican and Founder
Victoria, British Columbia

THOSE WHO OPEN craft breweries in Canada start off as avid beer drinkers, but all seem to eventually end up as experts on navigating laws and bureaucratic rules. When Paul Hadfield and his then partners John Mitchell and Ray Ginnever opened Spinnakers, Canada's first brewpub, in 1984 they had to work through three levels of red tape. In particular, federal excise laws at the time prohibited the sale of alcohol from the same building in which it was brewed—the whole point of a brewpub. By working to change these laws, Hadfield and his partners made one of the cornerstones of craft beer in Canada possible.

In the early 1980s, the Canadian beer market was dominated by three large companies, so the partners knew that if they wanted to sell craft beer it would have to be as part of a whole gourmet experience. Eventually they built a guest house and shop to sell the products of the in-house chocolatier bakery. With his training as an architect, Hadfield went to work finding a site and designing the buildings while Mitchell worked on a way to import the brewing equipment they needed from England.

As the retail market for craft beer has grown, they have recently added a canning line and steadily increased brewing capacity. More markets for their product and a new brewing facility will give the brewmasters the opportunity to experiment with different styles, including sours and barrel-aging.

At Spinnakers, unlike almost every other brewery, they intentionally encourage their beer to turn to vinegar. The artisan vinegar-making operation produces a diverse range of carefully crafted malt vinegars. In their controlled commercial system, a bacterium called *Acetobacter* is introduced to the beer, and it turns the alcohol in the beer into acetic acid. Each style of beer produces a different flavour of vinegar. (Spinnakers' process is faster, but the concept is essentially the same as the one behind the recipes for making vinegar in this book.) The full range of malt vinegars is for sale from their on-site shop.

As a Victoria institution it's not surprising that Spinnakers was invited to open a satellite location at the Victoria International Airport when the airport was renovated in 2012. Both food and craft beer from Spinnakers are available to the travellers who will join locals as devoted fans of the brewpub.

BEER COCKTAILS

Before I wrote this book I didn't really go in for beer cocktails. They reminded me too much of white wine spritzers—of taking a carefully made drink and making it haphazard. Not much about cookbooks is controversial, so I won't exaggerate the point. I think it's fair to say that often the idea of craft beer and cocktails clashes. We recognize (sometimes venerate) the work that goes into creating craft beer, and that makes it seem wrong to mix it with strongly flavoured ingredients or even to dilute it with ice.

Through some careful experimentation, I've developed recipes that emphasize the delicious flavours in the beers without overwhelming them with sweetness. Most of the cocktail recipes are calibrated for one serving, but can be easily scaled up for a larger party. There is something to be said about the conviviality of one pitcher of cocktails for everyone and it makes organization easier for the host.

RADLER

RECOMMENDED BEER
Pilsner
Traditional Pilsner, Creemore
    Springs Brewery (Molson Coors)
    (Ontario)
Pilsner Urquell, Plzensky Prazdroj
    (SABMiller) (Czech Republic)

SERVES 1

....

2 cups (500 mL) sparkling
lemonade

2 cups (500 mL) pilsner

lemon wedge, for garnish

THIS COCKTAIL COMES with an amusing back story. In 1922 the owner of a country pub outside of Munich is overrun with a crowd of "bikers" so large that he worries he'll run out of pilsner. Thinking quickly, he cuts the beer with sparkling lemonade and everyone goes home happy. Great yarn, but the drink was probably invented by 1912 and "radler" is German for cyclist.

Some sources allow the use of lemon-lime soda like 7UP or Sprite, but I really think it pays to find a sparkling lemonade that isn't quite as sweet. Making your own sparkling lemonade is also a great excuse to use that seltzer maker you bought years ago and haven't used since the novelty wore off.

German tradition makes up for the diluted alcohol by serving radlers in 1-litre (1-quart) steins.

———— ⟫⟩⟨⟪ ————

Chill both the lemonade and beer very well. Combine in equal proportions and serve in large mugs or tall glasses. Garnish with a lemon wedge.

Shandy Gaff

WITH PICKLED GINGER

RECOMMENDED BEER
Ginger beer and English-style pale ale
Ginger Beer and Blue Buck, Phillips
   Brewing (British Columbia

SERVES 1

1 cup (250 mL) ginger beer, chilled

1 cup (250 mL) English-style pale ale, chilled

pickled ginger for garnish

IN THE UK a shandy is roughly the same as a radler, except that there is an even greater chance it will be made with lemon-lime pop rather than lemonade. The shandy gaff, though, is its predecessor and is traditionally made with ginger beer.

A resinous and strongly aromatic English pale ale and a spicy Caribbean-style ginger beer do each other the favour of calming their partner's rough edges. Phillips makes an excellent alcoholic ginger beer. If you can't find it, go for a good-quality non-alcoholic ginger beer rather than an inferior hard one.

There is an interesting contrast between the warm spiciness of a good ginger beer and the cool, cutting edge of pickled ginger. Rather than force your fellow imbibers into the hassle of trying to dig a piece of pickled ginger out of the bottom of their pint glass, do as every sushi restaurant in North America does and just serve it in a dish on the side, please.

———— ⫸⫷ ————

Fill a pint glass to just a bit over the half-full mark with ginger beer. Top with pale ale and serve with pickled ginger on the side.

GIN AND TONIC

SERVES 1

....

2 oz (60 mL) Plymouth gin

tonic water to taste, but not more
than 6 oz (185 mL)

2 dashes Hop Extract (page 160)

lime wedge for garnish

PLYMOUTH GIN AND the flavour of hops go together like duelling electric guitars. Pine, citrus and spices are the obvious melody, but it's the complex, earthy bass line that is worth appreciating.

———— ❧ ————

Fill a highball glass halfway with ice cubes. Add gin and top with tonic water. Add dashes of hop extract to the cocktail's surface and garnish the rim with the lime wedge.

NOTE As with all cocktails, it's important to use fresh ice. So that the ice cubes don't pick up undesirable odours, it's best to store them in a closed container rather than open ice-cube trays.

BERLINER WEISSE

WITH RASPBERRY SYRUP

RECOMMENDED BEER
Berliner weisse
Nickel Brook Green Light Berliner
  Weisse, Better Bitters Brewing
  (Ontario)
1809 Berliner Style Weisse,
  Schlossbrauerei Au-Hallertau
  (Germany)

SERVES 1

....

2 cups (500 mL) Berliner weisse,
chilled

2 Tbsp (30 mL) raspberry syrup

RASPBERRY SYRUP

3 cups (750 mL) raspberries

½ cup (125 mL) sugar

½ tsp (2.5 mL) freshly squeezed
lemon juice

I REALLY APPRECIATE THE faint sourness of an unadorned Berliner weisse, especially as a substitute for a brunch bellini, but serving it with raspberry syrup (or woodruff syrup, an herbal essence that gives the beer a bright green colour) is traditionally correct. The syrup adds sweet balance and a beautiful colour. The idea of drinking it through a straw—as is the prevailing custom in Berlin—is a bridge too far for me.

If you have a favourite raspberry syrup, go ahead and use that, or make the recipe below ahead of time so that it is well chilled. The amounts listed will make enough syrup for 25 to 30 drinks.

———— ≫≫⫷⫷ ————

To make the syrup, set a heavy-bottomed, medium saucepan over medium-high heat and pour in all of the ingredients. Cook for 6 to 8 minutes, stirring frequently, until the fruit has lost most of its shape and the water is a juicy pink-red. Take the pan off the heat and let stand for 15 minutes.

Line a sieve with cheesecloth and set it over a large measuring cup. Transfer the raspberry pulp from the pan to the sieve and let the syrup drain into the cup. Collect the edges of the cheesecloth, bring them together and twist the bundle to wring out as much juice as possible.

Transfer to a tightly sealed container and store in the refrigerator for up to 3 to 4 weeks.

To prepare the cocktail, coat the inside of a chalice glass with a schuss (German for "shot" or "large dollop") of raspberry syrup. One of those clear squirt bottles that TV chefs are fond of is a helpful and inexpensive (though optional) tool for this. Fill the glass with chilled beer.

DARK AND STORMY

RECOMMENDED BEER
Ginger beer
Propeller Ginger Beer, Propeller
   Brewery (Nova Scotia)

SERVES 1

....

1⅓ cups (340 mL) ginger beer
(1 small bottle), chilled

2 oz (60 mL) dark rum

SOMEWHERE OUT THERE, right at this very moment, a booze company is paying a PR firm and a hired-gun "mixologist" to develop a cocktail recipe that they hope will be permanently connected to their brand. A staggering majority of these connections will never stick, but one that did is Gosling's Black Seal Rum and the Dark 'n' Stormy. The Bermuda-based rum company has trademarked the cocktail's name (at least without the "a" and "d" in the middle) and has sued to enforce it.

This is another version of the recipe, made with the non-alcoholic ginger beer from Propeller Brewery, but it would work as well with an alcoholic ginger beer like the one from Phillips that is recommended for the Shandy Gaff with Pickled Ginger (page 150). The hot-weather and nautical associations speak for themselves here: this drink goes down perfectly as the sun slips below the yardarm on a hot August afternoon.

Put 3 or 4 ice cubes in a highball glass. Add ginger beer and top with rum.

Black and Tan

RECOMMENDED BEER
English-style bitter or stout
(bitter) London Pride, Fuller's Griffin
    Brewery (United Kingdom)
(stout) Aphrodisiaque,
    Microbrasserie Dieu du Ciel!
    (Quebec)

SERVES 1

½ pint (250 mL) bitter

½ pint (250 mL) stout

THE BEST-LOOKING beer cocktail—really an experiment in fluid dynamics—is also delicious. Black stout is carefully floated on top of less dense, amber English-style bitter. The one gets its bitterness from roasted malts, the other from hops, and the combination is an exercise in subtle contrast.

The black and tan is what the most devoted stout drinkers turn to on insufferably hot days when a thick-as-coffee drink seems a bit much. The roasted malt flavours from the stout go well with so many salty-meaty summer foods (grilled sausages come to mind) that this drink deserves a regular spot in the rotation.

The name is controversial in Ireland because there it also refers to the Royal Ulster Constabulary, the government police force that kept order during various 20th-century conflicts in Northern Ireland. But in the rest of the world it's descriptive and the most recognizable way to order a stout-and-bitter.

———— ❂ ————

Half fill a pint glass with bitter. Hold a soup spoon with the convex side facing up over the top of the glass and pour the stout gently onto the spoon. To maintain the visual effect, serve gently.

NOTE There are purpose-designed spoons with an abrupt "U" in their handle that hooks over the rim of a glass. I hope it goes without saying that this tool is not at all necessary for the home cocktail-maker.

"GLØGG"

RECOMMENDED BEER
Winter ale
Winter Warmer, Garrison Brewing
(Nova Scotia)
Underlig Jul, Nøgne Ø (Norway)

SERVES 4-6

COOKING TIME 15 minutes

4 cups (1 L) winter ale

2 cups (500 mL) unsweetened apple cider

8 green cardamom pods

peel of 1 orange

2 cinnamon sticks

grated cinnamon for garnish

GLØGG IS A Scandinavian Christmas drink in the same spirit as mulled wine. Here is my version of the drink, naturally featuring craft beer. The idea for this recipe came from one on Nøgne Ø's website. They are the most widely known craft brewery in Norway.

Set a heavy, non-reactive pot over medium heat and pour in the beer and apple cider. Add cardamom pods, orange peel and cinnamon sticks. When the gløgg comes to a bare simmer, reduce heat to low and cook for 10 minutes so that the spices can infuse the liquid with their flavour and aromas.

Serve with a dash of grated cinnamon on top.

NOTE If you can find a fairly dry version, hard apple cider is an acceptable substitute for the soft unsweetened apple cider.

BUTTER BEER

RECOMMENDED BEER
Scotch ale
Iron Duke Strong Ale, Wellington
   Brewery (Ontario)

SERVES 4

COOKING TIME 15 minutes

. . . .

4 cups (1 L) Scotch ale

¾ tsp (4 mL) freshly grated nutmeg

½ tsp (2.5 mL) ground ginger

¼ tsp (1 mL) cloves

4 egg yolks

½ cup (125 mL) sugar

2 Tbsp (30 mL) unsalted butter,
cut into four cubes

THIS IS A convivial drink for those of us who don't belong to the eggnog fan club. It needs to be served warm, straight from the pot.

More than four centuries before J. K. Rowling devised her band of child wizards, the British made butter beer to warm frosty winter evenings. In true Tudor fashion, it was spelled inconsistently, often with an extra "e" on the end. The Tudors were comparatively strict about the distinction between unhopped ale and hopped beer. Historical recipes are clear that the recipe was always made with ale very low in hops.

———— ❭❭❭❬❬❬ ————

Pour the beer into a medium saucepan and set it over medium-low heat. Use a probe or candy thermometer to monitor the temperature. Add the nutmeg, ginger and cloves to the pan.

Meanwhile, with a hand-held mixer, beat the egg yolks and sugar until the colour and texture are noticeably lighter. When you turn off the mixer and lift the beaters, the mixture should fall off the beaters in ribbons.

When the beer reaches 120°F (50°C) remove the pan from the heat. While whisking constantly with one hand, pour the egg yolk and sugar mixture into the pan with the other hand. Return the pan to the burner and boost the heat to medium. Continue to stir the butter beer constantly until it thickens slightly, about 2 minutes, maintaining its temperature between 160°F and 170°F (71°C and 77°C). If it climbs above this range, you'll likely end up with a pot of scrambled eggs floating in beer, that taste vaguely of Christmas.

Off the heat, give the drink another minute of vigorous whisking to froth the surface. Serve in festive cups or mugs, dropping a cube of butter into each.

THE PANTRY

This section has the "beer pantry" recipes—the condiments you'll want to serve with some of the recipes earlier in the book, as well as with your own special dishes. These recipes also experiment with the interesting flavours from beer ingredients, such as hops.

It's a shame that we don't use hops more often in recipes. As well as that bitter kick that cleanses the palate, hops bring a variety of fresh, often citrus-like flavours and aromas to recipes.

As I wrote the recipes that call for hops, I faced the recipe writer's usual problem: I don't know very much about you. I hope that at least a couple of the hands holding this book have also been put to work making home-brewed beer. For the most part, there is really no reason to draw a firm line in your head between brewing ingredients and cooking ingredients. Obviously, yeast as one of the principal ingredients in bread has the least trouble crossing this divide. Malted milk powder and the ice cream malts that shared a heyday with the soda fountains of the early 20th century are the closest food to feature the grains normally used in beer. Hops were cultivated as a spring green before they landed solidly in the beer ingredients category.

Hops are sold by homebrew suppliers from their stores and websites.

HOP
EXTRACT

MAKES 1 cup (250 mL)

PREPARATION TIME 10 minutes, plus at least 1 week to extract flavours

⅓ oz (10 g) pellet Centennial hops (about 3 Tbsp/45 mL)

1 cup (250 mL) vodka or other neutral grain spirit

WITH THEIR GENERAL bitterness and grapefruit flavours in particular, American hops have a natural similarity to cocktail bitters. The jump from pint glass to bar shaker is a short one.

Hop extract is the defining ingredient for the Hopped Gin and Tonic (page 151), but it also makes a great addition to food recipes that need a bit of bitter balance.

Place the hops in a 2-cup (500 mL) Mason jar or other glass container with a tight-fitting lid. Pour in the vodka. Let steep in a cool, dark place for 1 week.

Line a fine-mesh strainer with cheesecloth and set it over a 4-cup (1L) measuring cup. Pour the liquid through the strainer. Force all of the extract from the hops by pressing on the solids with a wooden spoon.

Clean the Mason jar and pour the hop extract back into it. Seal tightly and store in a cool, dark place for at least a week before using. The extract will start to lose its finer citrus notes after a few months.

NOTE Cascade, Chinook or Citra hops would all make excellent substitutes for the Centennial. In a pinch you could use whole hops instead of pellets, but the problem is that they will suck up much more of the liquid and you'll have to pay more careful attention to pressing every drop out after the steeping stage. Also remember that whole hops will have a greater volume than pellets, so it's important to measure them by weight.

HOP

Salt

MAKES a bit less than 1 cup (250 mL)

PREPARATION TIME 10 minutes

....

1 oz (30 g) Cascade pellet hops

7 oz (200 g) kosher salt

THE IDEA OF flavouring salt is not a new one. Rosemary, lemon and vanilla all can be used to add interesting flavours to salt. A faintly bitter hit and citrus aromas are great for completing a dish. This salt will play equally well with subtle flavours like those in steamed whitefish and more robust ones like fried foods.

I use kosher salt because I want the coarse texture that makes sprinkling the salt easier and because I want to let the hops take most of the attention. Coarse sea salt would also work well, but the complex mineral flavours of fancy, unrefined versions may be obscured by the hops.

Many hop varieties will do a good job of infusing their flavour into salt. Aromatic ones that are earthy or citrusy like Amarillo, Challenger and Cascade are good candidates for first experiments.

Crumble leaves from dry hops into a clean spice grinder or mini food processor. Blitz until they form a fine powder. Combine in a small mixing bowl with kosher salt and stir to mix evenly. Transfer to a clean Mason jar and store tightly sealed. Hop salt won't perish, but the flavour and aroma will start to fade after a couple of months.

IPA

MUSTARD

RECOMMENDED BEER
American-style India pale ale
Boneshaker India Pale Ale,
    Amsterdam Brewery (Ontario
India Pale Ale, Southern Tier
    Brewing (United States)

MAKES 1 cup (250 mL)

PREPARATION TIME 10 minutes,
plus at least 4 hours to soak

....

scant ½ cup (125 mL) mustard
seeds

½ cup (125 mL) India pale ale

4 tsp (20 mL) vinegar (your own
beer vinegar is best, but cider or
white vinegars are fine substitutes)

1 Tbsp (15 mL) brown sugar

½ tsp (2.5 mL) kosher salt

¼ tsp (1 mL) nutmeg

MUSTARD IS WORTH making at home because it is relatively easy to customize and keeps for ages, and fancy versions can be quite expensive. Change the texture by varying the amount of whole soaked mustards seeds you reserve.

Mustard has a hot, slightly acid flavour so I think it's best to draw complementary bitter flavours from beer. That way, the mustard will contrast nicely with malty sweet pretzels or sausages bursting with salty juices.

Next-level brewing Jedis will want to ferment their own beer vinegar (pages 161–170) and use it for this recipe.

Soak the mustard seeds in the IPA for at least 4 hours or overnight.

Reserve a quarter of the soaked mustard seeds. In a mini food processor or blender, combine the other three-quarters of the soaked mustard seeds with the vinegar, sugar, salt and nutmeg. Blend for 1 minute or until most of the seeds have lost their individual texture. Fold the reserved seeds into the mustard.

Pack into a scrupulously clean Mason jar, seal tightly and store in the refrigerator. The mustard is ready to use right away, but will only get better with a few days to rest, and should last for at least 4 to 6 weeks.

MUSTARD

RECOMMENDED BEER
Pumpkin ale
Pumpkineater, Howe Sound
   Brewing (British Columbia)

MAKES 1 cup (250 mL)

PREPARATION TIME 10 minutes,
plus at least 4 hours to soak

....

a scant ½ cup (125 mL) mustard
seeds

½ cup (125 mL) pumpkin ale

4 tsp (20 mL) vinegar (your own
beer vinegar is best, but cider or
white vinegars are fine substitutes)

1 Tbsp (15 mL) maple syrup

½ tsp (2.5 mL) kosher salt

PUMPKIN ALE IS one of the most popular entries in the calendar of seasonal craft beer styles. Just as with pumpkin pie, it's hard to say how much of the flavour comes from the gourd, and most versions could more accurately be described as "seasonal autumn spice ale." That's fine and we can use it to our advantage to make a mustard that is slightly sweet and accented with warm spices.

Soak the mustard seeds in the pumpkin ale for at least 4 hours or up to overnight.

Reserve a quarter of the soaked mustard seeds. In a mini food processor or blender, combine the other three-quarters of the soaked mustard seeds with the vinegar, maple syrup and salt. Blend for 1 minute or until most of the seeds have lost their individual texture. Fold the reserved seeds into the mustard.

Pack into a scrupulously clean Mason jar, seal tightly and store in the refrigerator. The mustard is ready to use right away, but will only get better with a few days to rest, and should last for at least 4 to 6 weeks.

TARTAR
sauce

MAKES ½ cup (125 mL)

PREPARATION TIME 10 minutes

¼ cup (60 mL) Hop Mayonnaise
(see page 166) (or mayonnaise)

¼ cup (60 mL) yogurt

2 Tbsp (30 mL) finely diced
cornichons

1 Tbsp (15 mL) capers, chopped

5 chive sprigs, minced

5 tarragon leaves, minced

½ tsp (2.5 mL) dry mustard powder

¼ tsp (1 mL) cayenne

1 tsp (5 mL) lemon juice, freshly
squeezed

kosher salt to taste

TARTAR SAUCE HAS been typecast as the partner for fish 'n' chips. Especially when lightened by the yogurt and its familiar twang in this recipe, I think tartar sauce goes just as well with grilled or poached fish.

Combine all of the ingredients in a medium mixing bowl. Taste and add salt or more lemon juice if needed. Leftover sauce can be refrigerated for 2 to 3 days.

HOP

Mayonnaise

MAKES about 1 cup (250 mL)

PREPARATION TIME 5 minutes

1 egg yolk

1 Tbsp (15 mL) water

2 tsp (10 mL) white wine vinegar

1 tsp (5 mL) Dijon mustard

3 pellets Cascade hops (optional), crumbled in a mortar and pestle

1 cup (250 mL) oil

kosher salt

JUST ABOUT EVERYONE who owns more than a few cookbooks or watches food television has heard from a choir of recipe writers and celebrity chefs that they should be making their own mayo. It is definitely worth the effort, but the usual technique of drizzling oil into the feed tube of a running food processor or blender is finicky and far from foolproof. On his blog *The Food Lab,* one of my favourite food writers, J. Kenji López-Alt, shared the idea of using an immersion blender instead. This method is quicker and much less likely to result in disappointment. If your mayo does split, just start with another egg yolk and use the split mayo in place of oil.

When hops are added to mayo to make "hoponnaise," their bitterness literally causes the mouth to water, making those salty, smoky and fatty foods—bacon or hot-smoked salmon, to name just two—even more addictively delicious. Without hops, this recipe will produce an excellent, traditional mayonnaise, but the flavour will be less complex and mouth-watering.

———— ✺≫≫≪≪ ————

In the tall plastic container that came with your immersion blender (or a 1 L Mason jar or other tall, narrow, clear container) combine the egg yolk, water, vinegar, mustard and hops. Gently pour the oil into the container and wait for 10 seconds until it settles to the top.

Before turning the blender on, put it all the way into the container so that the blade shield touches the bottom. Turn the blender on and run it in this position for 30 seconds or so until you see an emulsion form at the bottom of the container (it will look like mayo). Gently tilt the blender to pull oil into the emulsion. Lift the blender slowly upward until all of the oil is emulsified. Remove the blender. Season to taste with kosher salt and more vinegar, if needed. Store the mayo refrigerated in a tightly sealed container. It will keep for 2 to 3 weeks.

BEER VINEGAR

SHERRY VINEGAR, lemon-thyme vinegar: a new flavour of vinegar seems to insinuate itself into our cupboards every week. There are two reasons for this. Vinegar is a delicious, calorie-free way to add flavour to dishes, and any beverage containing alcohol can be converted into acid by *Acetobacter*. This is the bacterium that—roughly speaking—digests alcohol and oxygen, and produces acetic acid, the main component in vinegar.

Beer vinegar (also known as malt vinegar or alegar) is made from a liquid that is technically beer, but it isn't very flavourful. Not much attention has been paid to creating premium, delicious versions of malt vinegar; a lot more thought goes into producing sherry vinegar, wine vinegar and apple cider vinegar.

For the process of home vinegar–making, you need a "mother" (or "starter"). The mother in vinegar is a semi-solid collection of cellulose and bacteria (the good kind) that forms on the top of unpasteurized vinegar. The easiest way to introduce a mother-starter to your vinegar-to-be is to add some unpasteurized apple cider vinegar to beer. The Bragg's brand of unpasteurized vinegar is labelled as "with the mother" and is often mentioned in recipes as a preferred option. (See the Cultured Beer Vinegar and Faux-Barrel Beer Vinegar recipes, pages 168 and 170.) You can also create your own mother-starter. (See the Wild Beer Vinegar recipe, page 169.)

In beer vinegar–making, the beer needs to be exposed to lots of oxygen so that the *Acetobacter* can thrive and the volatile compounds contributed by the aroma, hops and yeast will dissipate or degrade. If you want to experiment with different styles of beer to produce different vinegars, it's best to focus on styles that get most of their flavour from their malt ingredients. Bocks, American and English brown ales, and Scotch ales all make great starting points to experiment with beer vinegar.

Homemade beer vinegar is excellent for more than just fish 'n' chips. In particular, it makes a great addition to salad dressing and can be used in homemade mustard. (One caveat: Never use homemade vinegar for sealed-jar canning. The safety of that process depends on using vinegar that is at least 5 percent acetic acid. Home cooks almost certainly do not have the expensive tools needed to accurately test the pH of their homemade vinegars. Litmus paper is not a safe option.)

CULTURED BEER VINEGAR

MAKES 1 cup (250 mL)

PREPARATION TIME 10 minutes, plus 10–14 days

¾ cup (185 mL) beer

¼ cup (60 mL) unpasteurized apple cider vinegar with mother

IN THIS RECIPE, a small portion of cider vinegar is used to inoculate the beer with *Acetobacter.* For batches after your first, you can use established beer vinegar that has an active mother floating in it in place of the apple cider vinegar. Before measuring the apple cider vinegar, shake the bottle to evenly distribute the mother.

Combine the beer and apple cider vinegar in a very clean 2-cup (500 mL) Mason jar. Stir to combine and swirl the jar to introduce as much oxygen as possible to the liquid. Cover the jar's opening with a thin towel, three layers of cheesecloth or a cotton handkerchief. Choose a material that is solid enough to keep flies out, but porous enough to let air in. Wrap an elastic band around the rim to hold the fabric in place.

Store the jar in a dark cupboard and check on it every few days, swirling the liquid each time to introduce more oxygen. Start tasting after 8 days and stop the process when it tastes as sharp as apple cider vinegar. The cultured vinegar should be ready after 10 to 14 days. If it isn't ready after 14 days, give it one more week, and if it still hasn't turned to vinegar, discard and start again.

NOTE Once the liquid has turned to vinegar, it can be kept in the refrigerator indefinitely, but the usual common-sense rule about food applies—you should not eat anything that looks or smells foul. The liquid should smell sharply of vinegar, but if mould appears or a stomach-turning aroma develops, discard the vinegar.

WILD BEER VINEGAR

MAKES 1 cup (250 mL)

PREPARATION TIME 10 minutes, plus 2–3 weeks

1 cup (250 mL) beer

ONE POSSIBLE DOWNSIDE to the cultured version of beer vinegar is that it retains some of the parent vinegar's properties (it will taste and look a bit like apple cider vinegar). An alternative is this recipe, in which "wild" *Acetobacter* is captured and used to create your own vinegar mother. The process takes a bit more time and is slightly less dependable, but the final flavours will be only those that are present in the beer and that were produced during the alcohol-to-acid conversion. To varying degrees, just about every environment has enough *Acetobacter* floating in the air to spontaneously convert the alcohol in beer into acetic acid.

———— ❧ ————

Pour the beer into a very clean 2-cup (500 mL) Mason jar. Stir and swirl the jar to introduce as much oxygen as possible to the liquid. Cover the jar's opening with a thin towel, three layers of cheesecloth or a cotton handkerchief. Choose a material that is solid enough to keep flies out, but porous enough to let air in. Wrap an elastic band around the rim to hold the fabric in place.

Store the jar in a dark cupboard and check on it every few days, swirling the liquid each time to introduce more oxygen. Start tasting after 14 days and stop the process when it tastes as sharp as apple cider vinegar. Wild vinegar can take 2 to 3 weeks to sour. If it isn't noticeably more sour after 21 days, give it two more weeks, and if it still hasn't turned to vinegar, discard and start again.

NOTE Once the liquid has turned to vinegar, it can be kept in the refrigerator indefinitely, but the usual common-sense rule about food applies—you should not eat anything that looks or smells foul. The liquid should smell sharply of vinegar, but if mould appears or a stomach-turning aroma develops, discard the vinegar.

FAUX-BARREL BEER VINEGAR

MAKES 1 cup (250 mL) beer vinegar

PREPARATION TIME 10 minutes, plus 10–14 days

....

¼ cup (60 mL) unpasteurized apple cider vinegar with mother

small handful wood chips (maple or oak are best)

1 cup (250 mL) beer

BARREL-AGING PLAYS an important role in traditional vinegar-making processes. Historically, barrels were the most convenient storage vessel. These days, producers of high-quality balsamic vinegar choose to age their product in oak because compounds in the wood will add subtleties and calm some of the harshness. By soaking wood chips in unpasteurized apple cider vinegar, we can culture the beer and add wood flavour at the same time. Before measuring the apple cider vinegar, shake the bottle to evenly distribute the mother.

————— ✦ —————

Pour the apple cider vinegar into a non-reactive glass bowl or pie plate. Add the wood chips and let stand until most of the vinegar has been absorbed, at least 1 hour.

Transfer the soaked chips to a very clean 2-cup (500 mL) Mason jar. Pour in the beer. Swirl the jar to introduce as much oxygen as possible to the liquid. Cover the jar's opening with a thin towel, three layers of cheesecloth or a cotton handkerchief. Choose a material that is solid enough to keep flies out, but porous enough to let air in. Wrap an elastic band around the rim to hold the fabric in place.

Store the jar in a dark cupboard and check on it every few days, swirling the liquid each time to introduce more oxygen. Start tasting after 8 days and stop the process when it tastes as sharp as apple cider vinegar. Cultured vinegar should be ready after 10 to 14 days. If it isn't ready after 14 days, give it one more week, and if it still hasn't turned to vinegar, discard and start again.

NOTE Once the liquid has turned to vinegar, it can be kept in the refrigerator indefinitely, but the usual common-sense rule about food applies—you should not eat anything that looks or smells foul. The liquid should smell sharply of vinegar, but if mould appears or a stomach-turning aroma develops, discard the vinegar.

HOP SHOOTS

MAKES 4-cup (1 L) jar

PREPARATION TIME 10 minutes, plus 1 week to mature

COOKING TIME 10 minutes

....

2 cups (500 mL) water

2 cups (500 mL) malt vinegar (or apple cider vinegar)

¼ cup (60 mL) sugar

1½ Tbsp (22.5 mL) kosher salt

8–10 black peppercorns

1 tsp (5 mL) coriander seeds

6 allspice berries

2 garlic cloves, peeled and crushed

large bunch hop shoots, trimmed to 1 inch (2.5 cm) less than the height of the jar

SOME HOMEBREWERS I'VE talked with took up their hobby to save money (taxes are a huge part of the retail price of beer in North America) or because they couldn't get the styles of beer they like in their market. But many (maybe even a majority) homebrew at least partly because experiencing the process enhances their understanding and appreciation for craft beer. It makes sense that some of these do-it-yourselfers will dig even deeper and try growing their own ingredients. From the general ingredient list of barley (or other grains), yeast and hops, the last is by far the easiest to grow on a small scale.

If you plant a hop rhizome this spring, you'll find next year (and every year after that) that you have more shoots than you want. The extras need to be trimmed and shouldn't be thrown away, because they are perfectly edible. Their flavour is much subtler than the cones and have a texture and shape that is often compared to asparagus.

Because hop farming has become so industrial and centralized, it's almost impossible to find hop shoots for sale. If you don't grow your own, or if hops are out of season, you can use asparagus, green beans or even small carrots instead.

I've calibrated this recipe to produce one large jar of pickled shoots that will need to be refrigerated, but will last well for about 6 to 8 weeks. If you'd rather preserve your shoots longer, they should be processed by hot-water bath canning. Sarah Hood's *We Sure Can!* and Linda Ziedrich's *The Joy of Pickling* have guidance on canning. (See Further Reading, page 176.)

Combine the water, vinegar, sugar and salt in a medium saucepan set over high heat. Meanwhile, very lightly crush the peppercorns, coriander seeds and allspice berries under a heavy pan. Transfer the

METHOD CONTINUES . . .

crushed spices and garlic cloves to a very clean 4-cup (1 L) Mason jar. Pack the hop shoots into the jar so that they are standing up. When the brine reaches a simmer, pour it into the jar to just barely cover the tops of the shoots.

Cover loosely and let cool to room temperature before tightening the lid and refrigerating. The flavour will be best starting after a week, and they should be eaten within 6 to 8 weeks.

NOTE If you want to use homemade beer vinegar for this recipe, do not process the jars (to seal them), and refrigerate and use the pickled shoots within 6 to 8 weeks. If you want to process the jars for longer storage, use distilled or apple cider vinegar that you know is at least 5 percent acid.

PICKLED

onions

MAKES 2-cup (500 mL) jar

COOKING TIME 1 minute

PREPARATION TIME 15 minutes,
plus 3 to 4 days to mature

....

2 cups (500 mL) pearl onions
(10 oz/300 g bag)

½ cup (125 mL) water

1½ cups (375 mL) Beer Vinegar
(pages 167–170), or malt vinegar or
white vinegar

⅓ cup (80 mL) sugar

2 tsp (10 mL) kosher salt

1 tsp (5 mL) celery seed

5–6 black peppercorns

pinch red pepper flakes

I'M IMPRESSED BY recipes that are brave enough to call for pearl onions in our age of hyper-convenience and momentary attention spans. Boeuf bourguignon comes to mind as a perfect example. Easily half of the active time and effort for the recipe is for the onions. If it weren't for Julia Child (and Julie Powell), I don't think any North American would ever make this dish.

The one time that I can muster the energy for pearl onions is when they're going into a brine for pickled onions. The convenience of having a jar in the fridge for weeks justifies the effort. Pickled onions are at their best with charcuterie and sandwiches, or in meat dishes like Steak and Ale Pie (page 109). As a pub staple and occasional member of a ploughman's lunch, they are a long-established partner for flavourful beer. The brine's sourness and the onion's heat match well with the malty and bitter flavours of craft beer.

Bring a large pot of water to a rolling boil over high heat. Have a large bowl filled with water and ice near the stove. This ice-water bath will be used to shock the onions after they come out of the boiling water.

Cut the root and stem end off each of the onions. Immerse the onions in the boiling water for 60 seconds and then use a spider skimmer or wide slotted spoon to transfer them to the ice-water bath.

While the onions are cooling, prepare the brine. Set a medium saucepan over high heat and pour in the water, vinegar, sugar and salt. Stir to combine and bring to a simmer. Remove from the heat.

Remove the onions from the water. Squeeze each onion gently from one end. The flesh should pop out the other end, leaving the skin behind. In some cases you may have to use a paring knife to help remove the skin.

METHOD CONTINUES . . .

Place the celery seed, peppercorns and red pepper flakes in the bottom of a very clean 2-cup (500 mL) Mason jar. Add the peeled onions to the jar and pour the hot brine over top. Cover loosely and let stand to cool to room temperature, a few hours. Tighten the lid and refrigerate the onions. The flavour will improve after 3 or 4 days and the onions will last in the fridge for at least 8 weeks.

NOTE Reusable plastic lids are the best option for refrigerator pickles. The acid in the brine can corrode the inside of the two-piece metal lids. If you use homemade beer vinegar for this recipe, do not process the jars (to seal them), and refrigerate and use the pickled onions within 6 to 8 weeks. If you want to process the jars for longer storage, use distilled or apple cider vinegar that you know is at least 5 percent acid.